To: Rife

SOUL IS WATER PROOF

ADVENTURE SWIMMING AND STORIES OF WATER

By
Matthew L. Moseley

Just Add Water.

[signature]

Soul is Waterproof: Adventure Swimming and Stories of Water

Written by Matthew L. Moseley
Edited by Elaine Howley
Proofread by Griffin Mill
Book design provided by Nicole Wurtele

All photos courtesy of Matthew L. Moseley unless otherwise noted.

Published by CG Sports Publishing

A Division of The CG Sports Company
cgsportspublishing.com

ISBN: 979-8-9881891-1-4
Quantity order requests can be emailed to:
Publishing@cgsportsmanagement.com

Printed in The United States of America

WHAT PEOPLE ARE SAYING:

"The human body is typically 60% water and perhaps that explains the connection that Matt has to water. In *Soul is Waterproof*, Matt shares inspiring and meaningful stories of his remarkable journey in water and in life. Especially in these days of climate change with increasing floods, droughts, and water extremes, Matt's stories will give you a new perspective on water and the majority of who you are too."

– Tom Kiernan,
President and CEO of American Rivers

"One of the world's most accomplished open water swimmers."
– *Outdoor Swimmer Magazine*

"Readers of *Soul is Waterproof* by Matt Moseley will receive a lesson in leadership and sustainability through the lens of experiential education. As Moseley shares his swimming adventures from around the world, it becomes clear that water has much to teach us about our fragile planet and its survival. The combination of experiencing what type of leadership it takes to navigate these very different rivers, lakes, and seas and understanding how water differentially affects the lives of populations throughout the world is a unique way to illustrate the impact of water on the survival of the earth."

– Philip P. DiStefano,
Chancellor, University of Colorado Boulder

"Authentic. Perceptive. Poetic. Matt provides a unique perspective on water, whether you are a policy wonk or an exercise enthusiast."
– Matt McKinney, co-director of the Water and Tribes Initiative, director of the Center for Natural Resources and Environmental Policy at the University of Montana.

"Moseley takes us on a journey through the centuries and around the world to examine our collective relationship to that most essential element, water. More than a mere travelog or adventure story – but certainly full of adventures! – *Soul is Waterproof* is a reminder to take nothing for granted; to live life to the fullest and take good care of what matters most: the people and resources that make life possible."

– James Edwards

"Soulful storytelling by an Ambassador of Water, *Soul is Waterproof* joins at a confluence rich, diverse characters such as John Wesley Powell, Sarah Thomas, Hanya Yangihara, Lord Byron, and Captain Matthew Webb, among others illuminated by Moseley's torch. Relationships with the essence of life, amidst anthropogenic climate change, are the current of this book. I imagine Coco Robicheaux blessing it—perhaps water, as a spirit, too."

– Jason Robison,
Professor, University of Wyoming College of Law;
Editor, *Cornerstone at the Confluence: Navigating the Colorado River Compact's Next Century and Vision & Place: John Wesley Powell & Reimagining the Colorado River Basin*

"Matt Moseley passionately and gracefully takes us with him to understand the priceless treasure that is water. Through stories, observation, self-reflection and humor Matt teaches us how to value what we have taken for granted for so long; the water that makes all of our lives possible. *Soul is Waterproof* reminds us what is essential to live and in relationship with the world around us."

– Rosalind Wiseman,
author, *Queen Bees and Wanna Bees* (the movie *Mean Girls*)

"You don't have to be a swimmer to dive into this book. You can float on the prose or ride the currents of adventure. If you ride the wave of *Soul is Waterproof*, you will emerge on the shore refreshed and invigorated."

– Mark Gerzon, author, *The Reunited States of America*

"Matthew seamlessly connects incongruent topics - unprecedented swimming adventures down rivers, across lakes, and in turbulent seas with historical facts and profound literary passages. His experiences point out mankind's need to adapt and survive in a world that increasingly has either too much or too little water in too many places. His voice rings loudly to those who listen, but his message is also a prophetic warning to those who may not."

– Steven Munatones,
Founder, World Open Water Swimming Association

"Humble and fascinating. I love the way Moseley connects with water and music through his amazing swims. Through his adventures and weaving of history, he develops a unique spiritual relationship with the bodies of water he swims in. If you love water the way we do, you'll love this book. If not. Prepare to be converted."

– Ram Barkai,
Founder and Chair, International Ice Swimming Association;
author, *From Fire to Ice*

"Moseley takes readers on a tour-de-force, deftly weaving together adventure, environmental conservation, history, spirituality, and downright "grit." *Soul is Waterproof* draws you in, captivates, and keeps you. Until it is over. Will the journey be completed? What does Moseley experience along the way? Why are the rivers of the American West – the Green and beyond – in this state? And what role does culture play in crafting experience, landscape, desire, individual and collective tenacity and hope? As an anthropologist, a resident of the West, and a deep believer in the transformative power of experience and storytelling for teaching us about people and place, I recommend you immerse yourself in *Soul is Waterproof*. You won't emerge the same."

– Colleen Mary Scanlan Lyons,
Ph.D author *Running After Paradise: Hope, Survival, and Activism in Brazil's Atlantic Forest*

"Matt Moseley has not only transversed some of the most noted—and treacherous —waterways in the world; he has used those lessons to navigate a pathway through the even more complex waves of human interaction."

– Christopher Tidmore, *Louisiana Weekly*

"Water is life and caring for our rivers, lakes, and the ocean are now more important than ever. I have been on a support boat with Matt as he swam through the night and into the following evening. He loves swimming, but it's more than that - it's about a love affair with water."

– Vicki Nichols Goldstein,
Founder and Director, Inland Ocean Coalition

"Matt's passion and commitment to water preservation is infectious. He delivers a message that is inspirational, aspirational, and important."

– Bart Foster, author *Business Outside*

"What Matt is swimming is mind boggling. The physical commitment and logistics are nuts. But maybe we need some level of human craziness to make people realize there is a growing, huge problem with our water and rivers that supply it."

– Pete McBride,
***National Geographic* photographer and journalist**

Also by the author:

Dear Dr. Thompson

Felony Murder Hunter S. Thompson
and the Last Gonzo Campaign

Ignition

Superior Communication Strategies
for Creating Stronger Connections

TABLE OF CONTENTS

PART ONE

PART TWO

PART THREE

This book is dedicated to everyone
who has ever been on the support boat and part of the crew.
To all those who picked up a paddle
stayed up through the night
through sunrises and sunsets
who were there through good times and bad.

For everyone who said, 'Yes!'

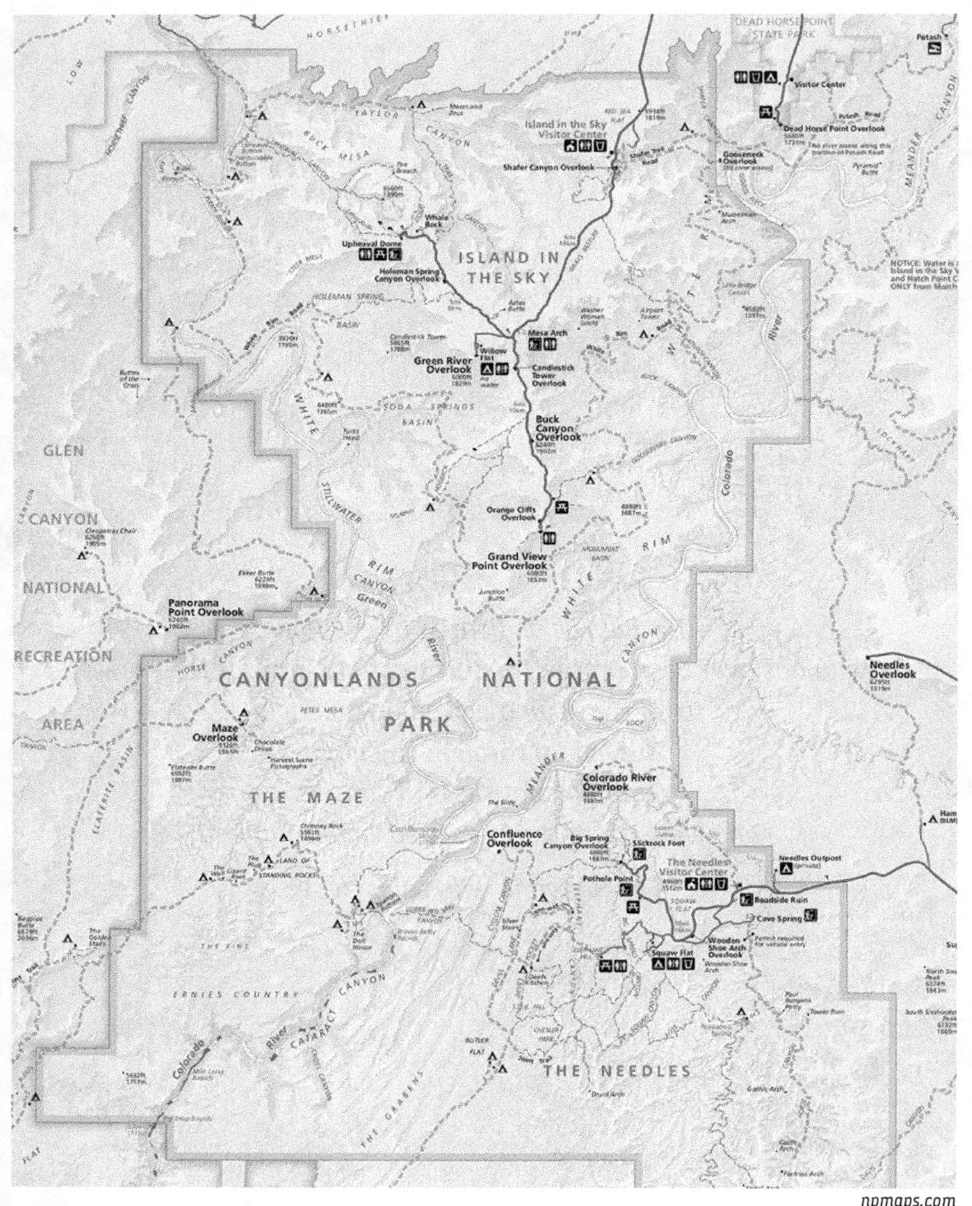

npmaps.com

Map of Canyonlands

PART ONE

The face of the water, in time, became a wonderful book—a book that was a dead language to the uneducated passenger, but which told its mind to me without reserve, delivering its most cherished secrets as clearly as if it uttered them with a voice. And it was not a book to be read once and thrown aside, for it had a new story to tell every day.

– Mark Twain

CHAPTER ONE

LEAVING TERRA FIRMA

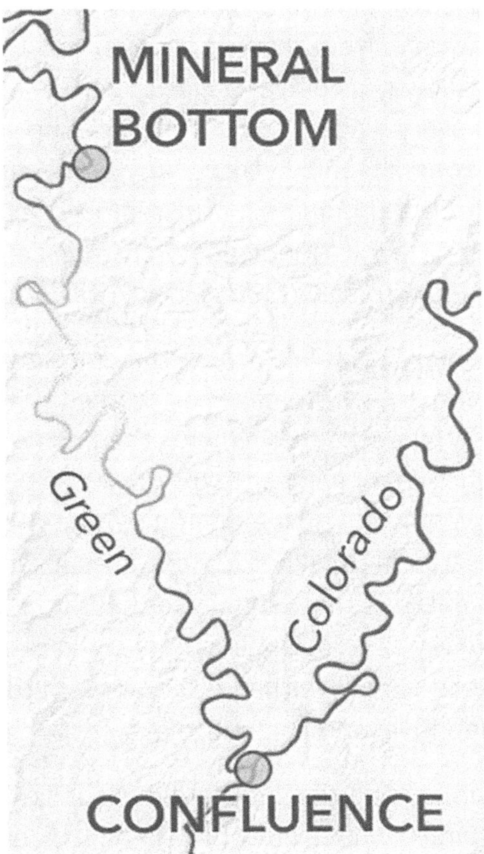

Mineral Bottom to Confluence of the Colorado River in Canyonlands

The first rays of sun crest the ridge at nautical twilight. Standing on the sandy riverbank in the early morning darkness, I prepare myself to do what's never been done before. At 4:54 a.m., droplets of fresh water float in my goggles. Nearby in the water my support kayak and canoe await, their blue and green rope lights glowing against the dark canyon walls. After years of planning, training, and soul searching, the moment has come to call.

The water I'm about to be swimming in, the Green River, begins as a trickle of snowmelt high in the Wind River Mountains of Wyoming and then gains force as streams from morainal lakes coalesce. By way of the Flaming Gorge reservoir, the river meanders south into Utah and the desiccated landscape of the Colorado Plateau. In its 40-mile bend into the northwest corner of Colorado it picks up momentum from the Yampa River and then returns to Utah. Along the way, the river builds character as it collects sediment. From every place it touches, it picks up something: dirt, specks of sandstone, organic detritus. Any bit of earth it can cradle in its flow—all flora and fauna—are invited. This little river carries a larger load of silt than its more glamorous partner, the Colorado River, and as a result its color changes over its course.

By the time it has made it past the churning twists of Desolation Canyon, the water has been worked to the richness of old leather, its surface shimmering with the fine natural sheen of a worn saddle. South of its namesake, the town of Green River, long a launching point for early river expeditions, the river continues to mellow. It loops around Bowknot Bend, traces a series of S-curves, and rolls along gently at about a mile per hour past the bank where I toss and turn in my tent, struggling to sleep in the final few hours before I attempt to complete the first-ever swim to its confluence with the Colorado River some 52 miles away.

I desperately need the shut-eye, but for some reason I can't get those wrecked cars out of my mind. Nearest access to the Green River is nearly an hour away from Moab, Utah, across long washboard dirt roads. A left turn takes one down a snaking ladder of switchbacks to the boat launch at Mineral Bottom. It's tough for big trucks and bus rigs loaded with boats and gear. Peering over, you can see the rusted remains of several cars that skidded over the edge, a harsh reminder to take it slow and easy. During the mining boom decades earlier, a number of truckers died on the perilous roads here. One poor guy was trapped when his bulldozer tipped over on him. Nobody was around, so to avoid a long, agonizing death, he freed himself by cutting off his arm with a pocket knife. No wonder I can't get to sleep.

The howling winds aren't helping my cause. With sustained gusts of up to 60 mph, the tent's rain fly flaps around and sounds as if someone is angrily beating an old rug. A tempest of swirling trees howls across the way, and high-pitched screeches fly around the canyon walls. Seems like every desert explorer had to contend with this wind. In 1869, Major John Wesley Powell, Civil War veteran and geologist, embarked on a 10-man expedition down this river to the Colorado and through the Grand Canyon to map the area for the U.S. government. Powell brought along barometers to measure altitude and a gifted writer's powers of observation and articulation. He recalls the beauty of his historic boat trip down, but also its challenges, "At night we camp on a sand beach. The wind blows a hurricane; the drifting sand almost blinds us; and nowhere can we find shelter. The wind continues to blow all night, the sand sifting through our blankets and piling over us until we are covered as in a snowdrift. We are glad when morning comes."

To pacify myself, I shift my thoughts to the beauty of my surroundings. There are few who are better at describing it than Powell, whose passages still reverberate among the canyons like the banter of those who accompanied him. Here he is detailing this very stretch of the river:

> *There is an exquisite charm in our ride today down this beautiful canyon. It gradually grows deeper with every mile of travel; the walls are symmetrically curved and grandly arched, of a beautiful color, and reflected in the quiet waters in many places so as almost to deceive the eye and suggest to the beholder the thought that he is looking into profound depths. We are all in fine spirits and feel very gay, and the badinage of the men is echoed from wall to wall. Now and then we whistle or shout or discharge a pistol, to listen to the reverberations among the cliffs.*

The figures of Powell and all who went before and after still live here. I saw them last evening in the rock formations, among other figures. I tend to see images in the rocks, such as Alfred Hitchcock in repose, the clouds billowing from his cigar. Faces, apparitions, and animal figures, mostly hidden among the boulders, reveal themselves at the oddest of moments.

I think of my evening stroll with a friend along the water I'll soon be swimming in. As the last rays of light hit the tops of the tawny walls, the canyon seemed to suddenly come alive: frogs croaking, bats swooping this way and that, searching for supper in the fading dusk. Perhaps in anticipation of the wind, the bugs, usually ubiquitous in this season, weren't on their hunt for blood. Heat from the earth released into vapors caused little wind bursts. After we extinguished our headlamps and our eyes adjusted to the evening light, the crunch of our footsteps gave measure to our conversation while stars popped out across the sky. Darkness fell, but it could not conceal the beauty. When the stars were out in full, they appeared to reflect the vastness of this canyon country. One could almost feel the earth rotating on its axis.

The noisy squall continues. It belies the quiet desolation here, which gives the impression these canyons are static and immutable. No. They are alive and ever-changing, and all the stories they've inspired before me testify to their dynamism. As does the wind. My thoughts are circling, which means I'm drifting off. Drifting up, that is. I have the sensation of levitating above the tent. Thoughts of explorers and images in canyon rock seem to have sent me spiraling above the tops of the cottonwoods. Such buoyancy belongs only to dreaming—and water.

The alarm goes off at 3:40 a.m. Nestled in the sleeping bag, I think, *Let me lie here forever*. The faint croak of a toad tells me that whether or not I've had enough sleep, the time has come, the game is on. I rise to make Community Coffee from my home state in the already-prepared-and-waiting French press and mugs. I eat a Bobo's Oat Bar, complete an all-important morning constitutional, and break the simple camp. As my three-person support crew prepares the boats, I change into swimsuit, goggles, and cap.

On comes the war paint: zinc oxide covers my body for protection from the sun on the long journey. My right arm is coated blue, my left arm red. My face is all white. *Red, Flesh, and Blue*, my support paddler calls it. This wasn't planned; these were the only colors available at the swim shop. For a second, I fear I look like a mime on the Fourth of July. But then I think, *One arm in fire, the other in ice*, and I'm reminded how this swim through a stark desert encompasses a slew of paradoxes. Hot sun, cold water. Conflict and calm. Adventure and monotony. A solitary endeavor dependent on communal support.

The instant toes move from terra firma to water is always the defining transition, as if descending into the netherworld. Water envelopes ankles, then knees. The chill travels up my spine through my neck to the base of the brain. *Hello!* The water feels silky, smooth. Viscous as heavy whipping cream. Three belly breaths come from deep within the core to fight off fear and nausea. The challenge right now is to control the emotions rumbling within.

After my knees are submerged, I give the Moseley Family Call. *Caw Cawhh! ... Cawwww Cawww* echoes back through the awakening rock.

I dive into the blackness.

CHAPTER TWO

LAGNIAPPE: A LITTLE SOMETHING EXTRA

As my strokes find purchase on the water, emotions swirl like the currents of the river itself. At first, I feel disoriented in the darkness. My long-time support paddler, Mark, falls into formation on my right side, the point of his kayak even with my waist. The nose of his boat will serve as my guidepost for the day. He knows just how important direction is.

After ten minutes or so, we settle into a nice rhythm. My stroke elongates and smooths out. The water is silty and murky. It has the faint taste of snowmelt, a bright, sharp steeliness with a slightly bitter aftertaste of sandstone. The canyon walls cruise by with every breath. At about 20°C/68°F, the river is chilly, but not too cold. Few realize this is a swimmer's paradise. With the current sweeping along, one can feel almost *Phelpsian.* Long and strong.

Toting just enough gear to keep us alive for two days, Mark skims alongside me in our 14-foot, two-person kayak. Meanwhile, Mike Fiebig has taken the helm as our lead navigator in tandem with videographer John Mans in the 14-foot Mad River canoe that stays not far ahead of us.

* * * * *

It's the same evergreen canoe I found awaiting me in the front yard years and years ago in Boulder, a birthday present from my then-girlfriend, Kristin. We didn't have much money in graduate school, so she had arranged for several friends and family members to chip in. The boat came with a trip down the Colorado River from

Moab, Utah, to the confluence of the Green River.

Kristin and I met in Telluride in 1991. She had come west from Michigan and had just finished an internship at the environmental newspaper, *High Country News.* I had come north from New Orleans. After three years in Telluride, we moved to Boulder, where she went to the University of Colorado Law School and studied water rights law. For several years, she worked as research assistant to the legendary Native American Tribal water rights attorney, Charles Wilkinson. I went to graduate school in public policy while working on a project for the Rockefeller Foundation. Looking back, I'd say our relationship was brewed in the Colorado River.

That first trip in 1995 with Kristin in the canoe 25 years prior may be the true origin of this swim. Amazing. And a complete disaster. We paddled an exhausting 65 miles in 6 days. We didn't bring shade, chairs, enough ice, beer, or anything really. We were totally unprepared for desert camping. But I did bring my swimsuit and goggles.

Those first swimming strokes on the Colorado River faded from minutes to miles. The strokes were liberating, glorious, open. In the river there were no lane lines, no clocks constantly clicking, no coach continuously coaching. Instead, swimming the river was free. Flowing. Independent. A completely different experience than I was used to in a box of chlorinated water. If swimming in a pool is like running on a track, then swimming in a river in a canyon is like hiking a forested trail. A sublime natural experience involving a startling paradox—feeling outside my skin, but within my core.

Kristin and I return to the river every year. Sometimes with friends, eventually with kids. These trips through Canyonlands, mostly by canoe, have become a formative experience for our family. In 1998, Kristin and I got engaged at the confluence. It's also where we found out Kristin was pregnant with our son, Charlie. Our children have developed a love for these river experiences that rivals their parents'.

* * * * *

Finally, the sun's rays reflect off the top of the canyon walls. Like the last drips of honey in a honey bear stood on its head, they slowly pour down to the bottom of the canyon. As the sun turns the sky pink and the morning begins to glow, I relax into my stroke.

Those who knew me when I was young would probably be shocked to hear I can relax at all. I was a hyperactive child. Sitting still and paying attention all school day long was nearly impossible for me. Today, a doctor would probably diagnose Attention Deficit Disorder. My parents introduced me to the swim team at the Lafayette Aquatic Recreation Club when I was 8 years old. They hoped swimming would calm me down and bring some regular breathing into the picture. Which it did. The swim practices burned off energy and wiped me out.

I swam through my junior year of high school. While I loved going to swim meets and the effervescent camaraderie that sprung up at these day-long events, it soon became evident that I wouldn't be going to college on a swimming scholarship. It seems some were even more disillusioned than I was. At one point, our long-time coach embezzled the team money and hightailed it to Costa Rica. The team struggled, and I drifted away and started drinking beer and smoking cigarettes. It wasn't until my mid-20s, when I was a graduate student at the University of Colorado in Boulder, that I came back to swimming for some of the same reasons my parents had initially enrolled me in swimming many years prior—to bring focus and clarity to my studies and general fitness.

If you hear "open water swimmer" and picture an Olympic-level, super-conditioned specimen, you'll need to adjust your expectations because that's not me. I haven't competed in any Ironman triathlons. One might describe me as a pleasantly chunky bon vivant. I like to hear live music and have fun with friends and family. I enjoy wine, vodka, and tequila. My demanding day job in public affairs and crisis communications often interferes with my training schedule, but I do what I can. Suffice it to say, I have priorities in my life other than swimming.

Because of my history, I consider myself a different kind of athlete, one with a unique approach to open water adventure swimming. My strength is not speed, but I can go and go and go. And keep going. Tortoise, not hare. Well, perhaps sea turtle.

I'm not the only one who's noticed that open water swimmers are a breed apart. In a 2016 *New York Times* piece, "A Brisk Swim Across Martha's Vineyard," author and swimmer Hanya Yanagihara describes the difference between the two types of swimmers. "You can either be very fast, or you can be very steady. Much the way you can immediately distinguish a ballet dancer (lithe, elegant) from a modern dancer (blocky, powerful), you can also immediately tell who's a speed swimmer and who's a distance swimmer. Speed swimmers look a bit like manta rays translated into bipedal form: long-torsoed, long-armed, short-legged. Distance swimmers are more seal-like: sleek, cobby, meaty. If you were a hungry shark on his daily glide, you'd eat the distance swimmer first." By that account, let's just say that during Shark Week, I'd be the chef's special.

Open water swimmers need a little something extra for protection from the cold. The great distance swimmers such as Lynne Cox, Martin Strel, and Sarah Thomas have different body types than world-famous swimmers we often think of, like Michael Phelps or Katie Ledecky. Whether one's body is suited to the pool or open water, whether we gravitate toward speed swimming or endurance swimming, all of us swimmers are fueled by an appreciation of water. Just as runners are by an appreciation of the ground beneath their feet; as cyclists are by the road beneath their tires; as skiers are by the snow they carve through. Olympic gold medalist marathon runner Frank Shorter and I once had this discussion in the gym locker room in Boulder. He told me that for lifelong athletes, "the body finds the sport it is most adapted to."

From those first formative strokes on the Colorado River, the swimming kept building. A one-mile race became a 5K (3.1 mile) race. I vividly remember my first 10K (6.2 mile) race on the Horsetooth Reservoir, not far from my home. After several of those, I figured, *Why not try the 12.5 mile Swim Around Key West*? Head down with some fellow swimmers—perhaps a few non-swimming friends as well—and have fun on the islands for a few days afterwards.

Out of nowhere, ideas for new swims start to appear. Some are challenges: *Hey, that lake's never been swum before.* Others are simply convenient. *Wouldn't a nice little swim in the Boulder Reservoir hit the spot right now?* And then there are swims born of circumstance. Perhaps, it's a swim across the sea with a friend who happens to have a boat. These ideas come to me all the time. Most just fade away. Some grab hold and won't let go.

After a time, the swims grew longer and more elaborate. *What if we swam six or seven miles on Lake Pontchartrain in New Orleans, made it a benefit, and then went to the Jazz and Heritage Festival afterwards? Ok. I know a riverboat bar pilot...*

My buddy's brother-in-law has a place on Lake Tahoe and a boat, so let's put together a relay team, swim 22 miles, and then all go to Burning Man...

Reality doesn't happen until we make it so. Until we say, *Yes.*

Those early swims imbued me with energy and endurance that grew over time. You might think you'd be exhausted from all the physical effort, but it's the opposite. At least, for me. After a big swim, the synapses are all ablaze. I'm clear and ready for an intensely good time with friends, music, and dancing. I feel *en fuego*.

For years, I partnered in these adventures with my cousin, Glynde Mangum—or Mango, as he's affectionately known. Our Ma Maws (grandmothers) were sisters from Oak Grove in northeast Louisiana. Mango's father, "Uncle Pete," was one of my father's best friends growing up and a hero to the whole family. When Uncle Pete played football for Ole Miss, everyone would gather around the radio to listen to his feats on the path to becoming an All-American. He was drafted to play with the New York Giants and then went on to play for the original 1960-61 Denver Broncos team.

Uncle Pete's family moved from Lake Providence to Houston, where he became a legendary high school football coach. (Think Coach Taylor in *Friday Night Lights*.) Glynde always excelled at swimming. He was an All-American swimmer at SMU, and while swimming in the finals at the 1984 Olympic Trials, just missed the US Olympic Swim Team in the 200-meter breaststroke. Mango has always been larger-than-life. Handsome. Fun. The biggest smile you've ever seen.

Because he's older and had moved to Japan after college, Mango and I were not acquainted growing up until we met in Boulder in the early 2000s. When my father attended Uncle Pete's funeral, he spoke with Glynde and mentioned I lived in Boulder. We eventually got in touch. Our energy immediately connected. Mango was the long-lost family member you finally discovered. We'd have become close, regardless of familial connection.

He'd just returned from over 12 years in Japan, where he'd been coaching the National Swim Team. For years, he was a professional triathlete sponsored by New Balance. He'd competed with the best in the world back in the founding era of Ironman Triathlon, when the historic races that played out between two of the all-time greats, Dave Scott and Mark Allen, defined the sport in the early days on NBC Wide World of Sports. Mango was third out of the water in the World Championship Hawaii Ironman Triathlon in Kona and a world-class athlete. Though I wasn't nearly as fast as him in the pool, we could still swim together. He was an inspiration in those early years.

He was also known for a particular incident in Seoul. During the 1988 Olympic games, Mango was out celebrating at the Hyatt Regency Hotel bar with Troy Dalbey, who'd just won two gold medals along with setting two world records. For whatever reason, they decided to *commandeer* a decorative sculpture in the shape of a lion's head sitting atop a fireplace mantel. The Korean police were called in, and they eventually caught up with our heroes at another bar. The pilfered sculpture was sitting in a chair and receiving toasts from the American swimmers, who alternated between downing shots and putting teeth marks in their gold medals. Arrested for theft of a historic artifact, they were kicked out of the country and off the team. A huge diplomatic and international incident ensued. Later, the story inspired a Trivial Pursuit card in the Sports and Leisure category. *What country saw two of its Olympic swimmers jailed after they were caught stealing a concrete lion's head from Seoul's Hyatt Hotel?*

Clearly, Mango's sense of adventure knew few bounds."Hey Mango," I'd say as the wheels in my head continued to turn, "I've got an idea. Why don't we go swim 15 miles on the Colorado River from the Moab Boat Ramp to Gold Bar, camp out, and then head into the Telluride Bluegrass Festival?" We'd spread the word to a few kindred spirits, make plans, set the date, and the next thing you know we're barreling down the highway with the windows rolled down, singing Led Zeppelin's "Ramble On" at the top of our lungs.

In our early years, we called them *Boondoggles*—trips of whimsy that combined a strong swim, a chance to gather a rollicking crew, and then an event where we could celebrate our achievement, such as a big festival or concert. That was the basic outline, anyway. We soon discovered that on these boondoggles, our actual experience tended to diverge from our more carefully thought-out plans. These escapades may have started as just little one-offs, ways to create a little adventure, but they slowly evolved into a lifestyle that has taken me to waters around the world.

I look back with fondness on all the memories, even the painful ones:

Swimming 8 miles in the Pacific Ocean from Sayulita to Punta de Mita, where I met the family. As I exited the water, a huge wave crushed me into the sand face-first. I lost my cap and goggles.

Crossing from Petoskey to Bar Harbor on Lake Michigan with Uncle Bob and Karel Howse in choppy waters in the low 50s.

Working as a press officer at the 2004 Olympics in Athens and swimming the Olympic triathlon course.

Bouncing in the waves in Valencia, Spain and waving at Charlie, who refused to be seen with me on the beach because I was wearing a Speedo. (Point taken.)

Cutting my leg on rocks swimming Kaanapali in Maui and trailing blood in the sharky water.

Getting stung by jellyfish swimming the Golfo Dulce in Costa Rica.

Burning my back and butt crack to a crisp as I crossed the Caribbean.

Running into a black snake near the I-10 bridge to Slidell on Lake Pontchartrain. It bumped against my head and slithered underneath my shoulder and down my belly. I thought it was a plastic bag, but the crew told me what happened. Someone yelled, "That poor little snake was just swimming along all scared and lost and you come along and run right over it!" I thought, *Wait... Whose side are you on here?*

Trying to pick up the pace during the 12.5-mile Race Around Key West, so that my assigned support paddler, a retired Navy captain with a ponytail and tactical knife strapped around his leg, could make it to Bare Assets, the strip club, for happy hour. "Only dollar beers and dollar lap dances!" We didn't make it.

Careful what you wish for. What sounds good one night after a few tequila shots might just happen. The dream starts to build and come alive. A date is set. And then you're locked in.

A Grand Traverse of the Colorado Plateau holds favor as one of our most memorable *boondoggles.* One person (Bud Thompson) would mountain bike the length of the Kokopelli Trail from Grand

Junction to Moab for over 120 miles (60 miles a day over sometimes rough terrain); then Jonathan Bartsch, and I would join Bud and together we would swim 18 miles on the Colorado River from the Moab Boat Ramp to Potash Point. (I tied the canoe around my waist and pulled all of our supplies and gear while we swam.)

Upon finishing the swim, we drove the White Whale, Bud's Suburban, to the North Rim of the Grand Canyon. After an unfortunate Taco Bell dinner, we rose at 3:00 am to run the 24 miles to the South Rim of the Grand Canyon, which was particularly difficult for me, not being a natural runner. Then we hopped back in the SUV and drove to Las Vegas to pick up Mango. After a wild night in Las Vegas, we pointed the White Whale towards Burning Man, 10 hours away, and the boondoggle continued and expanded, albeit in a different way. This trifecta across the American Southwest was one of those magnificent 2,000-mile midlife crises. They're not all bad, and I'm fairly sure the Grand Traverse hasn't been done before or since.

You take the good with the bad. I remember getting kicked in the face at the start of the 5K Open Water Swimming World Swimming Championships in San Francisco. I've also tangled with algae, jellyfish, the floating waste of nutria rats, mysterious things brushing against me in the night, water lice, lightning, fierce chop on the open seas, and storms. And some of the most magical and sublime moments a human could ever ask for.

* * * * *

Even though every water molecule is composed of two parts hydrogen and one part oxygen, not all water is the same. Water has a remarkable capacity to take on the characteristics of all it passes through. Given geography and geology, climate and land use, each body of water develops its own personality.

I've tasted water all over the world. Felt the viscosity. From brackish Lake Pontchartrain where the Mississippi River meets the

Gulf of Mexico, to the North Pacific of Hawaii, the Mediterranean, and the bluest blue of Lake Tahoe. I believe I have developed a rather sophisticated palate for the stuff.

Closing my eyes and smacking my lips I can taste water from the Boulder Reservoir. I recall *a deep chestnut, with notes of goose poop and a dumpster juice finish.* Then again, on the Colorado River maybe it's more of *a richly textured cappuccino, with a backwash of uranium tailings and a dash of Rocky Mountain gypsum.* Swimming with the ghosts of Ernest Hemingway on Walloon Lake in Northern Michigan where he spent his summers and wrote, the shimmering early morning a reflection of the verdant forests coming alive after the winter frost, the water tastes like kissing a newly unearthed emerald. Maybe the Court of Master Sommeliers would consider including water connoisseurs? If such highly trained professionals can employ such lofty descriptive adjectives to give meaning to fermented grapes, surely the intriguing substance of water deserves as much.

Hours of swimming in the salty ocean can leave your tongue feeling like you've been licking the back of envelopes all day. The water of the Moab Boat Ramp evokes the taste of a bleached bone found in the desert. Swimming in Destin and Pensacola I've picked up notes of fish scales and tarragon. Water from the Sea of Galilee brought to mind leavened bread. Lake Tahoe smacked of what I imagine chilled fine silk would taste like. The Red Sea felt like olive oil on the palette with afternotes of cardamom, rosemary, and crushed seashells. I've tasted iron and rust, rock and dust. A swimming hole in the Pacific Northwest offered a bouquet of forest floor. The water flowing from Rocky Mountain National Park into Lake Granby tastes evergreen, fresh, almost like fresh-cut summer grass.

But the best, purest water—like eating freshly fallen snow or splashing your face in a high mountain stream or plunging into the icy stillness of the deep Arctic Ocean—tastes exactly like nothing at all. The best water is clean and crystalline. The complete absence of flavor, what I imagine the Milky Way itself might taste like if you could reach your ladle into it. Just a little sip from inside the Big Dipper.

If you find yourself thirsty and parched after a long endeavor out in the sun for hours or even just coming home from a long day at work, drinking a tall glass of water filled with ice can be one of the most satisfying sensations known to the human body. The mouth, throat, and stomach can't seem to get enough. Gulps and gulps. Nothing tastes as good, and it tastes of nothing at all.

As opposed to ocean water, which can be sticky because of the high salt content, the water of the Green River feels soft and silky on account of the fine silt that travels from the tributaries from the Yampa River. It feels *inviting*, as if coming here has been an answer to being called, not merely in fulfillment of plans we've been making for years.

This would be my fifth major endurance swim (along with countless races). Five years prior, I swam the Colorado River for 47 miles to its confluence with the Green River in 13 hours. In many ways, swimming the Green River feels like completing the second half of that swim. So, that's why it's the Green River this time.

Another swim, another story. Another adventure, another memory. Only this time the stakes are much higher than with any of the other boondoggles. I'm older. I have sponsors counting on me. There's a professional cinematographer shooting all of this for a possible documentary. A photographer for *National Geographic,* is along. There is an app that tracks my progress in real time by satellite. And there are 16 people on the team waiting for me at the confluence. Afterward, we'll be rafting Cataract Canyon. Much time, energy, and training has been invested in this venture.

When I feel the pressure mount, I use a mental trick to *reinterpret*. It's not stress weighing me down, it's a force pushing me forward. It's momentum generated by taking all the steps to get me this far. Each of my swims is founded upon what I've learned by its predecessors. Building upon successes, compensating for failures, I've constantly tweaked, revised, and experimented over the years.

I'll confess I've always gathered inspiration from the idea of becoming a small part of history. It's not easy to go down in the record books these days. Most undertakings have been realized at this point—by somebody somewhere. The world is just too full of people. That's why I haven't done the English Channel or the big popular swims like Catalina Channel or the Swim Around Manhattan. All great accomplishments, but they are packaged experiences. The English Channel may have beautiful aspects, but it's oily and congested with ships, notorious for jellyfish and crazy currents. It has become the Everest of swimming. Expensive and overdone. (That said, I never rule anything out completely.) I'm after a different, more independent adventure. For me, the prospect of accomplishing something unprecedented, namely being the first to swim the Green River, gives me an extra energy boost.

As I take a breath and glimpse Mike Fiebig piloting our trusty green Mad River canoe out in front, the sight fills me with joy. The boat bears a few nicks and scrapes and its gunwales and seats have been replaced, but otherwise it's in as good of shape as it was the day Kristin surprised me with it for my birthday in '95. On that first trip down the Colorado all those years ago we christened the boat *Lagniappe* (*lan yap*), which means 'a little something extra' in Cajun French, where I'm from in Louisiana. Might be an extra donut or an extra pinch of jumbo lump crabmeat. Sometimes I think of those memories from the early boondoggle years—those late afternoons bathing in the dusk of a well-lived day, those starlit nights on the beach with close friends sharing what's most important to us—as a little dash of spice to give our lives extra flavor, extra frisson. The *Lagniappe* has certainly added a little something extra. I'm grateful for that canoe and, even more so, for the woman who brought it into our lives. We would not be here swimming the Green River without it.

CHAPTER THREE

THALWEG: STAYING IN THE DEEPEST CURRENT

So, how does a swim like this come together? Finding the right people for the right roles.

I pulled into a coffee shop in Aspen to meet Matt Rice from American Rivers, a nonprofit conservation organization, to prepare for a debate that night on whether or not to put a hydropower turbine at the foot of Maroon and Castle Creeks. It was 2010, and I'd been hired to run a campaign against public funding for the project. The Aspen Skiing Company, the big dog in town, was supporting the city and driving the pro campaign. The issue had become contentious.

As Matt and I strategized over coffee, Mayor Mick Ireland, dressed in cycling apparel, approached and launched into a tirade, "What the fuck are you doing here? We don't need you on this hydro issue."

Mayor Ireland and I knew each other from previous campaigns, and he could be emotional, volatile even. Then he started swinging his bike helmet around as if he were about to strike us with it, making a huge scene.

"Get out of our town!" he yelled.

Luckily, Sheriff Bob Braudis, an old friend who happened to be having coffee nearby, intervened and told Mayor Mick to chill. But then Sheriff Bob looked at me and Matt and shook his head. "Moseley, you've been in town less than an hour and you're already causing trouble?"

Welcome to the water wars of the West.

Even in the 1800s, Mark Twain realized how precious water is in the West when he remarked, "Whiskey is for drinking. Water is for fighting."

We prevailed in that campaign, and Matt has been a close friend ever since. We've worked on some contentious water issues together beyond Aspen, and we've passed funding ballot measures for the Colorado River and to fund the Colorado Water Plan. When I mentioned the idea of a swim on the Green River with rafting down Cataract Canyon afterwards, he jumped right in and put the full support of American Rivers behind it. While Matt and I have been tight for many years, somehow this was our first time on the river together. Years before the trip, Matt had told me, "I know just the guy to get us down the Green River and through Cataract Canyon."

One of his colleagues, Mike Fiebig, director of the Southwest River Protection Program for American Rivers, was recruited and assumed the role of leading our trip support and logistics. My swim, from Mineral Bottom to the confluence, accounted only for the first part of the overall trip. The second part, the rafting section with 16 people, would start at the confluence and go for another 47 miles through Cataract Canyon, one of the last remaining stretches of wild river in the West and some serious whitewater.

An eager, earnest Michigander, Fiebig is known for providing a constant stream of *Heck Yeah!*s and *Let's do it!* He exudes the good-natured jolliness and humor of a Canadian Mountie. *Here I am to save the day!*

As we began planning, Fiebig quickly became a trusted friend. He and I shared the long and lazy day before the swim, when there was little to do but rest and chat underneath the shade of the old cottonwoods of Mineral Bottom where Powell had also camped. I knew when I first started talking to Fiebig about the swim that he understood the scope and planning required. I continue to be grateful that Fiebig grasped what I was trying to do and was excited to be a part of it. As someone who had just completed a life-changing experience on the Green River himself—an historic Source-to-Sea raft trip—he appreciated the chemistry of the entire adventure.

A Source-to-Sea is the trip of a lifetime for anyone—from the very headwaters of the Green River, through Lake Powell, the Grand Canyon, and Lake Mead, to the end of the Colorado River. Fiebig and his wife, Jenny, a mental health therapist, had just finished the entire adventure in six months, following in Powell's steps. Along the way, they floated through the Flaming Gorge reservoir, portaged around the dams, and rafted the very section I was attempting to swim.

Fiebig has been on rivers most of his life. In addition to working for American Rivers, he's led expeditions, taught, and guided for a number of organizations including the National Outdoor Leadership School (NOLS). Fiebig started guiding in 1998, just after moving West. He has expeditioned on waters from the Arctic to the Andes, closing in on 20,000 river miles.

At American Rivers, every seven years, staff get a two- to six-month sabbatical. As Fiebig's sabbatical approached, he started thinking of various options for a long river trip and the one starting from the headwaters of the Green and continuing through the entire basin system seemed to be the logical choice. "If you love something, like the rivers on the Colorado Plateau," Fiebig told me, "you want to know all of it. Even the ugly parts. Every inch."

On the trip, he and Jenny explored all that the river is and all that it does. "The Colorado is a working river. We ask a lot of it." They also learned to see different perspectives after interviewing scores of people they met along the way: miners, county commissioners, park rangers, and a wide assortment of other river folks. "What surprised me the most is that partisanship falls away when you start talking about rivers, and especially the Green. There's this wonderful commonality that's rooted in connection to place," he explained.

Fiebig was describing the *topophilia* of what people felt about this river. They do not just live *near* the water, they are *of* the water. A deep connection and love of place. He explained what he discovered that surprised him and Jenny, "When you read the papers, everyone appears to be divided, but that wasn't what we found. When we asked people what the Green River or the Colorado River meant to them, nearly every person teared up. They spoke of the profound influence it's had on their lives. And every last one of them wants a healthy ecosystem and a good river. There's a lot of hope out there."

Along the course of any river, you encounter eddies, sandbars, holes, rock gardens, and other features. For an open water swimmer, these are obstacles. Smack dab in the middle of a river's course flows the *thalweg,* German for "valley way" or, to be exact, a path that follows the bottom of a valley. In legal terms, the thalweg of a river is the political line dividing countries, states, or neighbors. Here it refers to a river within a river. The thalweg is the deepest and fastest part of the channel. Fiebig's job in the *Lagniappe,* which was positioned in front of us reading the river, was to keep us in the quickest water. This would be critical to our safety and the success of our endeavor.

If at the center of the river you find the thalweg, at the center of this river swim you'd find Mark Williams, my stalwart support paddler. Every time I take a breath to my right side, there's Mark. One of the challenges in finding a good support person is their willingness to sit in a hard kayak, canoe, or boat for a very long time. There is little to no stopping and sometimes you're forced to figure out creative ways to do everything—from relieving yourself to continuing to concentrate on rhythmic stroke after stroke. As a former F-15 fighter pilot and one of the last to see man-to-man aerial combat over the skies of Baghdad when he was chased by a Russian MIG, Mark is not only uniquely equipped to sit his butt on a hard surface for 17 hours and keep his wits about him, but probably the most capable person I could possibly find to use the tip of the 14.5-foot orange Perception kayak as a beacon to guide my way.

Mark's training has ingrained an innate sense of staying in formation, which is more important than you might expect on a journey of this sort. Many paddlers drift out in front of me, even though I expressly tell them not to. They think they're leading me. But what I need most is to be able to sight off my support boat. When I breathe to my right, the nose of the kayak should be in the 3:00 to 4:00 position in relation to the top of my head and ideally six to ten feet off to the side. My swimming is directed by the kayak's bow, which points where to go. This way I can cut back on sighting (picking up my head and looking around to get a sense of my surroundings). Sighting takes energy, and over the long term it can be quite depleting. With Mark, I know I'm in good hands. When we're on the water he stays just as cool as he did when whizzing through the air on combat missions.

Mark and I have been friends for over 15 years. We first met on a congressional campaign. He was our foreign policy and military advisor. After retiring from flying, Mark started a career in artificial intelligence and later ran for congress. He also works with veterans who have PTSD, first responders, CEOs, and athletes on using meditation and mental techniques to enhance performance. He developed a powerful mental conditioning program that I practice to sharpen focus, enhance awareness, and settle the nerves. He's been by my side, both literally and figuratively, on most of my significant long distance swims.

As a communications strategist, I have honed my organizational skills over the years working on countless projects. Part of the job is to produce things, such as press conferences, speeches, rallies, forums, and all manner of events for causes and clients. Planning, building, coordinating the elements, working the plan, putting the pieces together—all vital, but nothing is quite as important as assembling *The Players*. On the Green River swim, my team was second to none. I should know, I've seen all kinds of support teams.

In the early boondoggle years, mishaps were always around the corner. I've had support teams show up late and extremely hungover after a night of hard partying with no sleep. When they did show up in the *Lagniappe* canoe, they ran straight over me. One year, one of the support paddlers in the two-person kayak, who was a tad larger, couldn't move the entire time so his legs went numb. At the end, he had to be helped out of the kayak and lifted by medics to regain circulation. While the race was another long, enduring marathon swim, it was my support team I worried most about.

At one point on my first 10K race on the Horsetooth Reservoir, I ran smack dab headfirst into a barrel marking the "No Wake" zone. Shocked and stunned, I discovered the support boat was gone. I turned and looked behind me to see the paddlers on the bank taking a whiz. *Come on, guys!*

Another time, during a different 10K race, I tossed the water bottle back to the *Lagniappe,* and when one paddler lunged for it, the canoe tipped over. I didn't say a word. Just kept swimming, following the shoreline for direction. I wondered if my support team would be OK. I wondered if I'd be OK swimming unsupported. Most of all, I wondered if they'd recover our beloved canoe? *For the love of God!* After maybe an hour, I saw the *Lagniappe* come paddling up. Turns out it had filled with water, and they'd nearly lost it. The Coast Guard lake rangers had to help them rescue the sinking canoe, which happened to contain the keys to my car—our ride home.

I've had many things go horribly wrong.

✲ ✲ ✲ ✲ ✲

For a while in the morning on the Green River I fall out of rhythm. Petty thoughts disturb my previous equanimity. I keep thinking about the keys we'd all hidden on the floorboard of our cars back at Mineral Bottom for the shuttle drivers. What if they can't find them? What if the cars aren't there at the take-out? We won't be able to get home. This needless little worry keeps buzzing inside my head like a gnat. Perhaps I'm fixating on the keys to avoid concerns even more relevant and unnerving.

In the lead-up to the swim, my twice-a-day training was not the only thing occupying my thoughts. There are real dangers that can come from swimming in a body of water for so long.

Nowadays, with information being so readily available, you can put faces to those dangers. There's the teenager in Devon, England, who was impaled (and nearly killed) when he swam into a rusty spike submerged below the surface of a river. The article I read about the incident included a quote from him that amounted to, "I didn't even know getting impaled in the river was a thing." And the local river conservation group was like, "Oh yeah, it's a thing, alright. Not uncommon at all."

Great. Very reassuring.

There's the 26-year-old professional open water swimmer who died during a race in Abu Dhabi. Medical experts believe the cause may have been heat stroke.

Wait, wasn't I, too, going to be swimming through a desert? In the heat of summer? At least, my water is cold, but that has dangers of its own.

Then there's the 39-year-old company president who suffered a fatal heart attack during a 1.3-kilometer swim in Lake Michigan. His vice president chimed in with shock and indignation, "He was not at all overweight. He ran regularly, he didn't smoke, he watched his diet. He was the last person I would think would succumb to an event like this." I think I read that one after ordering a third margarita to wash down the queso fundido.

Early on in the planning stages, Mike, Mark, and I had extensive discussions about the risks involved, including the usual suspects: cardiac arrest, hypothermia, disorientation, nausea, and vomiting. But it was the picture of blood streaming down from the deep hole just below the English kid's collarbone that gave me the willies. That was our worst fear: *Impalement*. And knowing that it could come at any time from any number of items—a submerged stick or a rock or industrial debris or jetsam—made it all the more frightening. We ran through various scenarios about what might happen if I were stroking along peacefully and then BAM! I got skewered in the face or the neck or the heart. That explains much of the terror caught in the back of my throat as my toes entered the water at the start.

Avoiding such a catastrophe was the main purpose of the *Lagniappe* lead boat. In a very real way, my life was in the hands of the support team. Keep in mind, we were in some of the most remote backcountry in the continental U.S.; a rescue wouldn't be simple. On the Green River, we were on our own, which is why navigation was critical. Trying to anticipate every circumstance, we had spent months talking about risk mitigation and had created a safety plan. Namely, we discussed the question: At what point—for what reasons—would the swim be terminated? And who would do the terminating?

We decided we didn't want to put anyone in danger by swimming long past sunset. When the light goes down and before the stars and moon come out, the sky gets ink-black in these parts. We would have light-ropes on the boats and headlamps, but they don't provide much long-range vision in the darkness of the enclosed canyon. We were not in a position to be equipped with high-powered spotlights and even if we had been, night swimming would still be extra dangerous. There were rocks and gravel bars, but my biggest fear was still of a hidden, submerged stick angling for the face, throat, or heart.

* * * * *

Of course, this time I was accompanied by no ordinary team. This was the very best collection of just the right people to come together for an expedition. I realized early on this swim must be pretty special to have all of these people take a week off work, use their summer vacation, find child care, and travel to Moab. The commitment from everyone involved in the trip continues to humble me. Even before hitting the water, I knew the assemblage of this team was the real treasure of the experience.

Many ask to be on the support team for my swims, but when they get a thorough rundown of what it actually entails, few pick up the paddle. I always try to be brutally honest about what it takes to be in the kayak next to me or on the support boat. The reality is that the experience is almost as grueling for the paddler as it is for the swimmer. The hours are long and intense. Unlike on that early Horsetooth 10K swim, you can't get out to stretch or even to relieve yourself. Apparently, Fiebig had to explain to John Mans how to pee in the bailing bucket (this was something I didn't telegraph). Especially in the ocean, we must feel like we're tethered together. If the tether breaks—and it has—there is real danger. This is no walk in the park.

Fiebig and I joked about creating a sticker that says, "Our best vacation is your worst nightmare," with a raven as our mascot.

How many people do you know who are willing to subject themselves to such adversity on someone else's behalf? How many times have you been recruited for such an undertaking? It takes special folks, indeed. When someone appears in your life who strikes you as right for your support crew, bring 'em on. Look for the qualities that Fiebig mentions when describing water people—be it lake, ocean, or river: Curious. Humble. Skilled. Hardy. Multifaceted. Prepared. Resourceful. Radically self-reliant. And my favorite, *Jovial*. Boat people get you where you want to go while minimizing friction instead of causing it. They deepen the experience because they exude a sense of quiet confidence.

The lesson applies to life, as much as on the river: Find people who are your *thalweg*—those who keep you in the deepest, strongest current.

CHAPTE

LEANDER'S LEGAC

Written After Swimming From Sestos To Abydos

If, in the month of dark December,
Leander, who was nightly wont
(What maid will not the tale remember?)
To cross thy stream, broad Hellespont!

If, when the wintry tempest roar'd,
He sped to Hero, nothing loth,
And thus of old thy current pour'd,
Fair Venus! how I pity both!

For me, degenerate modern wretch,
Though in the genial month of May,
My dripping limbs I faintly stretch,
And think I›ve done a feat today.

But since he cross'd the rapid tide,
According to the doubtful story,
To woo,--and--Lord knows what beside,
And swam for Love, as I for Glory;

'Twere hard to say who fared the best:
Sad mortals! thus the gods still plague you!
He lost his labour, I my jest;
For he was drown›d, and I›ve the ague.

– Lord Byron

I'm still feeling a bit off-kilter when Fiebig hollers at me. All along, the calculation is that at 3 miles per hour the entire swim should take about 17.5 hours. After swimming 11 miles on the

ass 'Outlaw Cabin,' built in the early 1900s. Mike o be slightly ahead of schedule, traveling about news gives me the energy boost I needed to ythm.

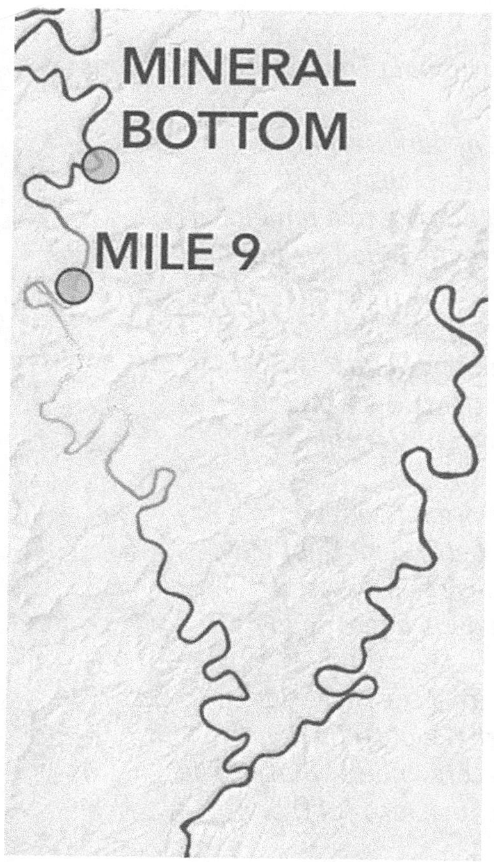

Mineral Bottom to Mile 9

Fiebig is also our official observer. Traditionally, marathon swims adhere to a slate of rules that attempt to pit the human swimmer against the elements with as little external support as possible. And it starts before the swimmer even enters the water. At the beginning of the swim, the swimmer must step off terra firma under their own power, and at the end, reemerge without supporting assistance from another person. During the entirety of the swim, the swimmer may not touch another person or the boat.

Swimmers are also limited in what they may wear to earn official recognition from any overseeing body. No wetsuits are permitted by traditional marathon swimming rules, also sometimes called simply, "English Channel rules." Rather, men can don a Speedo-style brief or a longer suit called a jammer that extends down the thigh but ends above the knee. Swimmers can wear one latex or silicone swim cap, a pair of goggles, sunblock or anti-chafing grease, and ear plugs or a nose plug, but nothing that aids in buoyancy or heat retention.

Steven Munatones, director of the World Open Water Swimming Association, or WOWSA, an acronym I particularly like, and the author of the defining book on the sport, *Open Water Swimming: Improved Performance for Swimmers and Triathletes*, explains, "As a matter of tradition, the rules refer to a solo swim or relay where the swimmers are not assisted, supported, or touched by other swimmers or individuals on boats, kayaks, or paddle boards, do not wear wetsuits, and continue unassisted from start to finish. The tradition of channel rules began with Captain Matthew Webb's successful crossing of the English Channel in 1875."

Webb is a hero of mine, not least because he was a fellow sea turtle—stamina over speed. On August 25, 1875, 27-year-old Webb became the first to cross the Channel, doing so in just under 22 hours. It was no surprise that an Englishman performed the feat—at the time, the English were known as the world's best swimmers.

Interest in open water swimming surged in 19th century Europe, and especially in England. Before then, Charles Sprawson, author of *Haunts of the Black Masseur: The Swimmer as Hero*, writes, "Almost no one swam in the sea. A few in the rivers. If there were exceptions, they tended to be aristocratic. Only those able to rise above popular superstition felt free to enter the water. Those who did were considered eccentric."

The Greeks and Romans celebrated swimming as a military art, but for them spending time in the water was a great pastime for a number of reasons: personal health, hygiene, and social engagement among them. Both civilizations built great pools and baths.

In Plato's time, it seems that a proper education included swimming. To call someone ignorant, he used an apparently common phrase, "The man can neither swim nor read." Back then, some regarded swimming as therapeutic. The Roman lyric poet Horace counseled, "Let those who are in need of deep sleep swim three times across the Tiber."

Swimming also made for dramatic escapes. In 48 BCE, besieged by Ptolemy's generals, Julius Caesar made a daring attempt to attack the island of Pharos. To beat back the siege, Caesar knew he would need reinforcements and that they would encounter resistance coming to port if his enemies controlled the famed Lighthouse of Alexandria, which stood on the island. When his attack failed and his boat was surrounded, Caesar jumped overboard and, holding aloft important documents, swam to safety. The legendary swim has inspired artists for millennia.

Caesar flees holding his Commentaries out of the water

Sadly, the aquatic history of the Greeks and Romans, in sport, leisure, and conflict would drown with the collapse of the

Roman Empire. Celebration of water would yield to a dark and ominous fear of demons and dragons that lurked in the depths. Swimming fell out of favor, and for over a thousand years it developed a reputation as being *unhygienic*, a vector for disease, and sinful, as the Church associated the bare flesh of swimmers with the mortal sin, lust.

A small revival would occur in 1587, when Everard Digby, a colorful, irascible theologian and Oxford Don, penned "The Art of Swimming." It was part inspiration, part instruction with a dash of common sense and a few safety guidelines thrown in for good measure. The treatise also contained 40 whimsical woodcuts depicting various methods of moving through the water.

Over a hundred years later, in 1696, the Frenchman Melchisedech Thevenot published *L'Art de Nager*, a text nearly identical to Digby's, complete with its own set of woodcuts. While Thevenot's book, essentially a knock-off, wasn't as significant as Digby's, which was reprinted numerous times throughout the years, it did have the good fortune of finding its way into the hands of a young Benjamin Franklin.

Franklin was a lifelong swimmer and loved the 'aquatic arts.' At age 11, he invented swimming paddles. He described them as "two oval pallets, each about 10 inches long, and 6 broad, with a hole for the thumb, in order to retain it fast in the palm of my hand. They much resembled a painter's pallets." Never quite satisfied with them, Franklin ultimately declined to mass-produce.

Perhaps you can imagine the wry amusement of the powdered-wigged onlookers when Franklin, who was in London working at a printing house in his early 20s, stripped and swam naked for three miles in the Thames one day in 1726. He was having so much fun teaching the aristocracy how to swim, America nearly lost its famous founding father. He considered staying in England and opening a swimming school. Good thing he'd already booked passage back to the Colonies.

Before and after Franklin's time, breaststroke was the most popular form of swimming. To Western sensibilities, its smooth, mostly splashless form seemed highly "civilized." Novice swimmers hoping to improve their form closely observed the motions of frogs swimming in troughs of water and imitated them. Webb used breaststroke to reach Calais. The effect that Webb's performance had on the English public should not be underestimated. Poet Algernon Charles Swinburne printed his reaction: "'What a glorious thing is this triumph of Captain Webb, and O what a lyric Pindar would have written on him. If only I could beg, borrow or steal the Theban lyre for half an hour I would try at an ode myself."

Pindar was not the only classical figure that Webb's triumph called to mind for admirers. Perhaps because of the way it combined human will, love, and tragedy, the myth of Hero and Leander played a significant role in the literary imagination of the Romantic period and served as a common reference. If you recall, Hero and Leander were young lovers who lived on either side of the Hellespont (today the Dardanelles), the strait in modern Turkey that technically separates Europe from Asia. Leander swam across the Hellespont every night, guided by Hero's lamp and propelled by the prospect of yet another tryst. Of course, it's the couple's tragic ending that immortalized them.

The September 4, 1875 edition of the famous British literary humor magazine, *Punch*, included an ode entitled "Webb Across the Water" that draws heavily on the myth. One stanza reads, "Leander was a Grecian youth, but Cap'n Webb's a Briton/Our Webb is to Leander as a large cat to a kitten/Or rather, since above all things a cat objects to water/Leander is a water rat to Webb, who is an otter."

If open water swimming could boast of a mythological godfather in Leander, then it could also point to two 19th-century patron saints. One, of course, is Webb. The other appears in the previous stanza of the *Punch* poem. "Hurrah for daring CAPTAIN WEBB, that resolute commander/He has far outdone Lord Byron,

Mr. Ekenhead, and Leander."

It's fair to say the craze for open water swimming began in earnest in 1811, when Lord Byron, the (in)famous Romantic poet, swam Leander's old lanes across the Hellespont with friend, Lieutenant William Ekenhead. Byron expressed more pride for this swim than he did for anything else he accomplished, including his long narrative poems, *Don Juan* and *Childe Harold's Pilgrimage*. In a letter to his mother, he wrote, "I plume myself on this achievement more than I could possibly do any kind of glory, political, poetical, or rhetorical."

Born with a clubfoot that forced him to walk with a painful gait his entire life, George Gordon Byron once confided in a friend, "I delight in the sea and come out with a buoyancy of spirits I never feel on any other occasion. If I believed in the transmigration of souls, I should think I had been a merman in some former state of existence." He swam all across Europe, and the locales have been marked for posterity. The sites include the bay between Portovenere and Lerici in Italy, a pond in Estremoz, Portugal, a stream between Portugal and Spain, the sea around Genoa, and in Venice the entire length of the Grand Canal. To the Venetians, he was the "English Fish." On one occasion, he decided to swim home after dinner instead of walking. Since it was night, he carried a torch in his left hand to warn the gondoliers to steer clear.

The image of that torch Byron carried above the surface of the canals recalls lines from his poem about Hero and Leander, *The Bride of Abydos* (Abydos, Leander's hometown, serves as an eponym for him). The second canto's opening stanza includes "Her turret-torch was blazing high… He could not see, he would not hear,/Or sound or sign foreboding fear;/His eye but saw the light of love,/The only star it hail'd above." I think of the torch as representing what we open water swimmers swim *for.* In the case of Leander, it was obviously love. Byron, I take it, swam for glory. The same could be said of Webb. My torch might be water itself, a counterforce of fire.

Webb continued the legacy of Lord Byron and the Romantics,

and, most importantly for posterity, his swim inspired the generally accepted rules of marathon swimming for decades to come.

Those rules, which were long unspoken but widely respected in marathon swimming circles, guided the sport down the ages and in waterways the world over. Those traditional rules governed William Wrigley's 1927 Ocean Marathon Race from Catalina Island to mainland California, won by 19-year-old Canadian newcomer George Young. Lynne Cox abided by these rules when she became the youngest and fastest English Channel swimmer at just 15 years old in 1972 and again when she rewrote all expectations of human endurance while swimming 1.2 miles in Antarctica in 2003. Sarah Thomas from Denver also followed these rules when she swam 104.6 miles nonstop in Lake Champlain in 2017 and when she broke the record for swimming the English Channel four times in a row nonstop, an 84-mile adventure she completed in 54 hours and 10 minutes in 2019, less than a year after overcoming breast cancer.

Webb likely never could have conceived of the distances some people are swimming today. Lynne Cox and Sarah Thomas are just two examples of swimmers going to great lengths in open water, and over the past decade or so, many marathon swimmers have notched eye-popping achievements in the world's oceans, rivers, and lakes. For example, Irishman and former rugby player Stephen Redmond was the first person to swim the Oceans Seven when he completed his final of the seven major channel swims in 2012. (The Oceans Seven consists of the English Channel, the Tsugaru Strait in Japan, the Catalina Channel between Catalina Island and the mainland of Southern California,, the Cook Strait between the North Island and South Island of New Zealand, the Molokai (or Ka'iwi) Channel between Molokai Island and Oahu Island in Hawaii, the Strait of Gibraltar, and the North Channel between Ireland and Scotland.) In 2018, Cameron Bellamy, a U.S.-based South African swimmer and no stranger to endurance adventures, became the 11th swimmer to complete the Oceans Seven. The following September he completed a 151.7-kilometer solo swim from Barbados to St. Lucia in 56 hours, 36 minutes, one of the longest ocean swims on record. And Webb likely never dreamed of the likes of Chloë McCardle, who has swum the English Channel solo a staggering 44 times and has set various distance records around the globe, including a 124.4-kilometer swim in the Exuma Sound in the Bahamas in 2014.

While some swimmers follow the strict protocols set by the Marathon Swimmers Federation, others make their own rules and swim in their own style. Martin Strel is one such adventure swimmer who holds several Guinness World Records for swimming the Mississippi, the Danube, and Yangtze Rivers. For the mother lode, Strel swam the entire length of the Amazon River, 4,345 miles over 66 days, with the aid of flippers and a wetsuit for health and safety reasons. Meanwhile, International Ice Swimming Association founder Ram Barkai, who is perhaps the most accomplished ice swimmer of all time, routinely swims in water that's right about at the freezing point without the benefit of a wetsuit. Though his swims in such temperatures seldom exceed a mile, they are still extraordinary examples of endurance in the face of extreme conditions.

There are millions and millions of people who swim everyday who are no less heroic. Those who make it to the pool despite circumstance, who overcome injury, who get in the water through good times and bad. From kids splashing to seniors stretching their limbs in the water; from Olympic athletes to beginners; from those who enjoy the pool to those who take to the open sea—all are tinder for my torch.

When I am training at the Meadows pool at the Aspen Institute, I always see the famous skier Claus Obermeyer, who swims every single day. He recently celebrated his 100th birthday. He told me one day that skiing and swimming are really not so different: they both require H_2O. Incidentally, this is probably my favorite outdoor pool anywhere because of its beautiful black tile bottom, salt water, and gorgeous mountain setting. Once, while swimming laps, I breathed to my right and saw by the edge of the pool a black bear just watching me go back and forth.

To be sure, there are many other open swimmers who have far surpassed my exploits, but I swim in the current of this same tradition, following the same rules that Webb did all those years ago. But within that framework, I'm out there creating my own stories. I'm pushing up against my own limits and bringing together my own people for a unique experience. Webb began a legacy: simple rules for profound adventures.

SWIMMING AND DYING

Sometimes when I'm swimming I think of nothing at all. I enter a Zen-like state in which cognition seems to cease and the act of rotating and breathing takes over. At other times, I think of *everything*. Often on my long swims, random thoughts flash through my mind.

As the rocks change colors with the ascending sun, some of my oldest memories come bubbling up.

The touching image of a cherished tin box in my closet filled with leather shoe polish and a brush my father gave me one Christmas. How he used to take me to all those swim meets so many years ago. My eighth grade science teacher, Mr. Gary Maurin, encouraging me to start cross-country running. Ms. Wanda Lemon, who coached me through Speech and Debate in high school. My first girlfriend. A road trip to New Orleans with Alan and Jay. A college party on a lake. Working as a counselor at Camp Hardtner, where the steam rose over the piney woods in the still-too-hot early mornings of Louisiana summer.

There appears the image of our family hunting camp, Katydid. If I could help it, I'd always find a cozy spot in the sun on the riverbank and watch the Mississippi roll by to avoid spending endless hours in some cold, dark hunting blind up a tree. As is natural for a kid who'd grown up on Mark Twain, I fantasized about taking a pirogue all the way down to New Orleans. I can still smell the old dank camp and that unmistakable aroma of squirrel gumbo simmering for days.

Memories continue to flash in succession as if fast-forwarding through the story of my life thus far. I imagine it's like what the movies have convinced us is that instant before passing to the other side, when our most precious moments come cascading through light.

The association between swimming and death is timeless. On the utterly barren Gilf Kebir plateau in the southwestern corner of Egypt, archaeologists study ancient pictographs in The Cave of Swimmers. Human figures painted on the cave's rock walls date back 10,000 years. They are horizontal bodies floating at different depths, which have been interpreted as the first human-made images of swimmers.

How paintings of what appear to be swimmers ended up in the middle of the desert, far from swimmable water, is still an open question, but climatologists have theorized that at the time, cooler weather and much more rainfall meant that the Saharan region was green with vegetation. A leading geomorphologist has discovered evidence of an ancient mega-lake that lies buried under the sand. Others contend that the painted figures are dead souls either floating in the netherworld or ascending to the heavens. I kind of like the ambiguity. Swimming can be like dying—and living. Descending and ascending. Transforming. Cleansing. Birth and rebirth all at once. Water, it seems, encompasses contradictions and resolves them.

The age-old association brings us back to the Hero and Leander myth. One night, high winds extinguished Hero's lamp. Leander lost his way and drowned. When Hero saw his lifeless body drifting to shore, she threw herself from her window to join him in death. If you look back at some of the greatest swimmers of the 19th century (and especially at the poets obsessed with water and swimming), Leander sadly seems to be a rather fitting model.

After his Channel crossing, Webb took advantage of his newfound celebrity by going on a lecture tour around the UK. He also tried his hand as inventor, patenting a unique form of a bicycle and a swimming contraption, complete with propeller. He painted—watercolors, naturally—and developed a reputation for being remarkably generous, albeit to the detriment of his young family. The years passed, and he went broke.

Webb concocted one final swim to end his career. One last heroic exploit: to swim across the notorious whirlpool just below Niagara Falls. His temerity made his friends anxious. Scores of people had died after accidentally getting swept into the dangerous stretch of river. No one before Webb was brave or foolhardy enough to attempt a crossing deliberately. Webb estimated that $10,000 was on the line from sponsors, money he desperately needed. Donning the same red silk trunks he'd worn during the English Channel swim that made him famous, Captain Webb dove off a boat into the Niagara River on July 24, 1883 at 4:00 pm. He held his course in the mid-channel as he entered the whirlpool. Spectators on shore watched intently as he swam into the center. Then they witnessed him suddenly throw up his arms and sink beneath the surface.

He shouted his last words to the boatman, "If I die, they will do something for my wife." Fishermen found his body several days later about four miles downstream below the falls, his red silk swim costume in tatters, his skull gashed. The illustrious hero of the English Channel now lies in repose in a cemetery at the edge of the Falls in a plot aptly called "The Strangers' Rest."

Byron too died young, but he managed to defy death in water. At 36, he succumbed to fever as he was about to join the Greeks in their resistance to Ottoman rule against the Turks. Until the end, he never tired of boasting about his swim across the Hellespont. In a letter to a friend, he emphasized the difficulty of it: "I swam from Sestos to Abydos, the immediate distance is not above a mile but the current renders it hazardous, so much so, that I doubt whether Leander's conjugal powers must not have been exhausted in his passage to Paradise."

To this day, Byron remains a hero to Greeks and a symbol of their fight for independence and the freedom of spirit. He was indisputably a strong, capable swimmer. His friend and fellow age-defining poet, Percy Bysshe Shelley, was not. Together they, like Webb, bear striking resemblance to Leander.

British biographer and friend of both Byron and Shelley, Edward John Trelawney described Shelley with a familiar comparison. He said Shelley "behaved as if he were a merman or a fish." In Byron's case, the merman comparison conveyed aptitude and affinity. In Shelley's, it spoke of a certain fatal attraction to water, an aquatic death wish. Sprawson writes, "One feels with Shelley that the inspiration behind his swimming was essentially classical — the devotion to water, the reading of Greek texts by Italian streams and waterfalls, his absorption in the myths of Narcissus and Hermaphrodite that suggest the enervating as well as seductive effects of water."

Before Shelley drowned in the sea off Viareggio, Italy, his inner circle often made note of how water bewitched him, drawing his focus from all else. He seemed to identify it as the only way to travel from this world to the next, and he'd stare down into its depths as if searching for signs of what was to come.

The allure of water is certainly romantic, sometimes erotic, almost sexual. French poet Paul Valéry described swimming as *'fornication avec l'onde,'* making love with the wave, a phrase which seems fitting in the cases of Byron and Shelley. And every surfer who's ever chased the perfect ride. Every diver who's frolicked among the coral reefs. Every rafter navigating the rapids. And every sailor on the open seas.

The poet Swinburne, who was so impressed with Captain Webb, also felt an intense allure, but whereas Shelley followed a narcissistic death instinct to the nearest pond, river, or bay, Swinburne took a masochist's delight in the power of the ocean. Sprawson considers the character, Herbert, in a novel that Swinburne never finished, as a stand-in for the author. At the seaside, "the scourging of the surf made him red from the shoulders to the knees, and sent him on shore whipped by the sea into a single blush of the whole skin." Herbert loves the brutal punishment: "He panted and shouted with pleasure among breakers where he could not stand two minutes the blow of a roller that beat him off his feet and made him laugh and cry out in ecstasy."

The Hellespont separated Leander from his lover. For him, water was an obstacle, an inconvenience. For open water swimmers, the challenge of the swim is the entire point. I'm not saying I share Herbert's fetish for the rough and tumble of the surf, but it's pointless to deny the masochism inherent in any big swim—in any extreme endurance sport, for that matter. I've been accused of being a masochist more times than I care to admit, though I don't necessarily think of it that way.

Sometimes I think I follow a torch that joins the flames that beckoned Leander and Byron and Webb. Love and glory together. I tend to fall back on the sentiment that Tennyson famously captured in *Ulysses*, another masterwork of the 19th century: "I cannot rest from travel: I will drink/Life to the lees... To strive, to seek, to find, and not to yield." Open water swimming is often called *endurance* swimming, and for good reason. There's something indescribably empowering about discovering all you can endure, all you can overcome, all you can do in spite of others' expectations, most of all your own.

Annette Kellerman, one of the great female swimmers of the early 1900s, dove from cliffs, swam in movies, and performed in exhibitions across the world. She created the women's one-piece swimming suit and aroused much controversy in the process. In her later years, she told a reporter, "I feel distance swimming is very important, not only as an exercise but as a character builder. Once you've accomplished swimming a great distance, anything else in the world seems easy by comparison."

There's more than love and glory to my torch, though. There's something transformative about it as well. Whether it's a regular team workout or an epic open water swim, the swimmer must prepare to be changed. Swimming, like good listening, or good living, requires being ready for all you may encounter and being open to being changed. The experience can be regenerative like a baptism or purifying like ablutions. A fresh start, a clean slate. If slipping into the water can be likened to death, then emerging from it is a kind of rebirth. Leander, Shelley, and Webb may have perished below the surface, but their legends endure.

* * * * *

When you're taking on a 52-mile swim, aches and pains and cramps and the rest are par for the course. You deliberately take it all on. Other times, pain and injury pop up without warning.

On my daughter Amelia's fourth birthday, we were coming off a six-day river trip on the Colorado River. We had to get going to make our dinner reservations at Pasta Jay's in Moab, but I wanted to get in one more jump off a cliff at Gold Bar before we left. Kristin encouraged me to check the water first. *Why?* I thought. We'd been jumping at the spot for over a decade. I slung myself over the 15-foot precipice.

Boom!

I hit a sandbar and shattered my right leg. I had to crawl out of the river and the mud to get back to the car.

Moab's hospital is basically a cinder block MASH unit filled with mountain bikers, climbers, dirt bikers, and dumbasses of other stripes who've wiped out and messed themselves up good. I was caked in mud and vaguely recall a doctor hovering over me and saying something like, "We can FedEx the parts from Grand

Junction and have you patched up in a few days." *A few days!* I chased some painkillers with a leftover beer from the cooler, propped myself up in the backseat, and we hightailed it six hours back to Boulder where I would get my own doctor.

I ended up with 17 screws and four plates holding the tibia and fibula together in my right leg and ankle. With all the hardware holding everything in place, the X-ray looked like the Eiffel Tower. The grainy black and white image made me sick to my stomach. People would look concerned and ask me what happened. I'd tell them, and they'd say something like, *Well, that sure was stupid.* So I stopped talking about it.

They were right, of course. Life suddenly turned inward in a stew of self-loathing. Words like *idiot* and *loser* kept circulating in my mind. Sometimes I would remember the impact itself. I realized how easy it would have been to end up paralyzed. Even dead. At least, Captain Webb had died in pursuit of making ends meet for his family. *What the hell had prompted my jump?*

The only thing I could do was learn my lesson: *Listen to your wife.*

PART TWO

CHAPTER FIVE

FOLLOW THE MERMAID: SWIMMING LAKE PONTCHARTRAIN

Swimming at sunrise on Lake Pontchartrain

After reconstructive surgery on my leg, I'd shudder every time I felt the plates and screws under my skin. It was a solid year of recovery with painfully intense physical therapy. Then all the hardware had to be taken out. Another eight months of recovery. All told, it was nearly two years. Oh, how I missed swimming.

That era was probably the most difficult time of my life. Doctors treat the injury, but they don't treat the mind or even address how your emotional state is affected by these injuries. Eventually, I had to make a decision: would I succumb to the injury and be defeated by it? Would I give up athletics and give in to the couch? Eat double portions, drink magnum bottles of wine, and get fat? Following the second surgery, the one that removed the plates and screws, I had to be careful not to get addicted to painkillers. I could see two channels emerging, like a river forking. One was dark and ominous. Down the other one, maybe a chance to rebound from the injury and create something greater in my life. A chance to become better than I had been before.

I had already begun working with Mark Williams on using mental conditioning techniques to sharpen my focus, feed my creativity, and stay disciplined when I shattered my leg. At that point, the mind game took on even more importance. It wasn't about climbing toward a higher place; I needed to ensure I wouldn't fall farther. I needed to avoid traps and pitfalls. I needed to manage the self-criticism and loathing that posed an even greater threat than the physical injury as they took hold and spread through my mind like a disease.

For a long time during my injury, I pushed away the leg. It was as if the appendage belonged to someone else. I put it outside myself so I could blame it for all the pain it caused. When Mark realized what was happening, he encouraged me to take the opposite approach. *Love the leg!* Bring it in and bathe it in light. The leg needs affection and tenderness to heal properly. I would later learn to apply the same lessons to other painful occurrences in life, not to push them away and retreat inside my turtle shell.

At some point near the end of the convalescence, a goal began to materialize. *What if I were to swim 25 miles across Lake Pontchartrain from New Orleans to Mandeville?* To me, it was unfinished business.

* * * * *

Four years earlier, in 2010, cousin Mango and I were going to New Orleans for the Jazz and Heritage Festival and decided to add a challenge to the front end of the trip. Another *boondoggle*. As a two-man relay team, we would be the first relay to swim across the lake alongside the Causeway, the world's longest continuous bridge over water. We knew risks abounded—alligators, bull sharks, strong currents, etc.—and so did every New Orleanian who heard of our plan. Their reactions hardly varied. *The lake? Why would you step foot in there?* An entire generation had come of age with NO SWIMMING signs posted all along Lakeshore Drive due to decades of industrial pollution.

My mother was more direct. "*Please don't,*" she pleaded.

But to be honest, the more people told us our idea was ludicrous, the more our enthusiasm for it grew. We got in touch with a few folks and before long the swim was part of a fundraiser for the reconstruction of the New Canal Lighthouse that had been destroyed by Hurricane Katrina.

Coming to the end of my rehabilitation three years after that two-man relay swim with Mango, I wanted to return to become the first known person to do that same stretch—25 miles—on a solo swim. I didn't just want to come back from the injury; in one indisputable way, I wanted to exceed our previous feat. For that reason alone, it felt like something I had to do.

This time, I met with John Lopez, executive director from the Lake Pontchartrain Basin Foundation (LPBF, also known as Save Our Lake) over a lunch of jumbo lump crabmeat salad on the lakeshore to discuss teaming up. LPBF was coming up on their 25-year anniversary of cleaning up the lake, so why not swim nearly 25 miles across it to celebrate and spread awareness and respect for this beautiful body of water? While we were at it, why not combine the crossing with music, art, and revelry? Most open water swims are fairly dull and drab, why not create a moving Mardi Gras on the water?

* * * * *

On the wall in my office studio behind my house there's a picture of Jack Kerouac, Allen Ginsburg, and Gregory Corso on a break from the filming of the Beat classic, *Pull My Daisy*. In the corner of the photograph is David Amram sucking on a lollipop. He had scored the music for the film. I met Amram while I was the communications director and family spokesperson for the Gonzo journalist Hunter S. Thompson's funeral and ash blast outside of Aspen. In one of our late night conversations, I floated the notion that Amram accompany me across Lake Pontchartrain and play music while I swam.

Of course! he said.

Amram has collaborated with such greats as Dizzy Gillespie, Thelonius Monk, Leonard Bernstein, Charles Mingus, Odetta, and Tito Puente. He scored *The Manchurian Candidate* with Frank Sinatra and is listed by BMI as one of the "Twenty Most Performed Composers of Concert Music in the United States." Amram didn't seem to mind (or realize) that the gig would entail playing keyboard and other instruments on a small party barge all night long and into the next day. At the time, he was 84 years old. There was no Green Room where he could relax. Heck, there wasn't even a bathroom. Having Amram committed to playing raised the stakes significantly. Suddenly, this was legit.

When I was just getting into adventure swimming on those early *boondoggle* swims, I relied on my good friend, Allen Buras, as my main support on the lake. Appointed Bar Pilot by the Governor of Louisiana, Captain Al brought big ships from the mouth of the Gulf of Mexico up the Mississippi River Delta into the Port of New Orleans. He knew these waters as well as anyone. He can navigate just about any boat in just about any condition. Finding a good captain was critical to the success of the trip, and in Allen we had not just the most capable captain on Lake Pontchartrain but a kindred spirit as well. Most boat captains aren't too keen about getting involved with a swimmer who doesn't wear a life vest. They try to prevent these kinds of situations, not encourage them. Allen, a triathlete, understood what I was doing.

It had taken about a year after my second leg surgery to build back to doing full workouts. Once I decided to get in shape I started doing sit-ups and exercises on the side of the pool after practice.

Swim coach Randy Soler approached one morning. In his thick Puerto Rican accent, he said, "Hey man... You training for something? You don't want to hurt yourself. How about a few suggestions?" And that's how I found my first personal coach. I had been swimming regular workouts with the Boulder Aquatic Masters (BAM) swim team for many years before, but I'd never had my own coach.

Randy believed in my mission. A great booster, he became a good friend. I soon discovered that a coach adds an extra level of accountability. I didn't want to let Randy down, so I worked hard. Sometimes perhaps a little too hard.

Six months before Pontchartrain, Randy wanted to take me down to Puerto Rico for a training swim. He introduced me to some wonderful people, and I fell in love with the country. We did a 14-mile swim on our first open water outing together. About one month before the Pontchartrain swim, I did my longest continuous workout ever—28,500 yards in nine hours in an indoor pool. At about 17 miles into the night, we shut off the lights and used only glow sticks at the pool ends to simulate night swimming.

Randy also had me doing dryland workouts outside the pool to build my overall fitness. Working out in the gym made me much stronger and helped to prevent injury.

* * * * *

I'd anticipated that the moment of diving into the dark night on Lake Pontchartrain would be unnerving, but as I stood on the shore of the shimmering, black water in the moments before my solo swim, one question turned my stomach. *What the hell had I done to myself?* When I arrived, I spied a place atop the levee where I could escape to try to harness the swirling emotions and focus on the singular task of making it across. I scrambled up, rolled out my towel, drank electrolytes, stretched, and then settled in for a meditation.

News teams gathered. The scene was reminiscent of Carnival. Two of the swim crew, Ryan Ballard and Richard Valadie, own businesses that design Mardi Gras floats. They provided a large merman, Neptune, strapped to the top of one of the barges. They illuminated the mascot, who stood bright against the night sky. That was the 'working boat,' with my friend, Allen Blow, behind the helm and George Ingmire, a DJ of the legendary radio station WWOZ, as our sound engineer for the musicians who would also play on that boat. Wayne Ewing, a documentarian I also met through Hunter S. Thompson, would be filming from this boat as well. The other was the 'navigation boat' with Captain Allen Buras, which stayed closer to me and guided Randy, who would be right next to me for feedings and sighting. Two or three other smaller boats followed behind like trailer fish. Moving across the lake at night under a nearly full moon, our parade cut quite the scene. I thought of the Neville Brothers singing, *Yellow moon. Yellow moon. Have you seen my Creole woman? Do you know something? Something that I don't know.*

Right before the swim, Wayne leaned close to me and said, "You've made such a circus around yourself, you have to make it." Perhaps he was right. By making such a big to-do about the swim, was I subconsciously raising the stakes to increase the chance of success? Whatever had inspired me, it didn't matter much now; the boats were readied and the television cameras were rolling. Curtis Robinson, our appointed observer, read the official WOWSA rules out loud, much the same rules that Captain Webb earned his fame following.

My torch was lit.

I carefully entered water the color of pitch. As I plunged beneath the surface, it seemed to move around me like a giant mass of sludge. It tasted slightly salty—the faint aftertaste of shrimp peel or oyster shell—the familiar taste that reminded me of all the other swims I'd done on this brackish lake. I was no stranger to these waters. I told myself I belonged here.

At first, we had trouble finding a groove, however. Nobody seemed to know who was following whom. I didn't need the full moon to show me we'd gone in a full circle. I raised my head in frustration.

"What's going on, folks?" I thought it had been clear from the get-go: Captain Allen Buras would take the lead on the upper left for direction, Randy would stay right by my side. The working boat with the musicians and film crew would be on the right past Randy.

"Let's all stay together!" I hollered.

We finally found our rhythm and began to work in tandem. David Amram was making up songs and having fun. *"Dancing in the water. With every son and daughter..."* The support crew was laughing and dancing to music, which fueled me with joyful energy all through the night.

Nine hours later, with the first pink hues of sun appearing above the lake, Randy stopped me quietly, which surprised me—it wasn't time for a feeding.

"Mateo, you've gotta see this."

David Amram was greeting the sunrise with a delicate melody on an oval Chinese flute that carried a deep resonance. The perfect score to a perfect scene: the earth's horizon materializing ever so gradually in the soft glow of morning. I shouted out to the boats, "This is why we came!" People shouted back, "Thank you for bringing us together!" and "We love you!"

In my whole life of swimming, that moment still ranks as the most beautiful and transcendent. I don't like to compare experiences because everything is so different, but it sticks with me even now. I can close my eyes and summon it to mind with all the sensory details to convince me I'm right back in the water, seeing the arc of the lake's horizon with all my friends on the boats.

I know that, for some, the image of the lake at night sends chills, but for those timeless hours, I felt snug in the dark water as if I were back in the womb. The night was soothing, not scary in the least. I had the moon watching over me, along with a whole crew of friends. The lights and lasers of the boats provided not just orientation but entertainment as well. Swimming along a vast lake with my own electric parade. Just before sunrise David Amram was joined by legendary musician Papa Mali and Alfred "Uganda" Roberts who was Professor Longhair's conga player. Now the music was infused with new energy.

Then the sun came up, and my world changed.

Rays of light splintered into my goggles. The glare of the early morning light gave me a headache. In the dark, I could hardly see the Causeway to my left, but in the plain light of day, it looked like its record for longest bridge in the world was well-deserved. It seemed to just stand still and not move at all. A breeze rippled the water, pushing it against me, enough to make things challenging. The going was getting tough, as I knew it would. I just didn't expect it to get so tough quite so quickly after the sun came up. I felt overwhelmed, and my fears came to call. For the first time, I thought about the bull sharks, the alligators, and the snakes.

Fear, not fatigue, may be the open water swimmer's greatest enemy.

SWIM, MY BROTHER, SWIM

For the relay swim on Pontchartrain several years earlier, in 2010, Mango and I decided that I'd swim the first half and he'd swim the second. The LPBF had signed on to this one as well and was throwing a big party at the New Canal Lighthouse when we finished. As he would be on the later solo swim, Captain Allen Burras was our stalwart pilot. Soft spoken and good-hearted, he had troubling news about the weather and wasn't about to put anyone in unnecessary danger. He delayed the original 9:00 pm start, and we waited it out at his place, a few miles from the boat launch. I was certain it wouldn't happen and started drinking chardonnay.

After monitoring the weather for a while, Capt. Al determined it didn't look too bad. He made the call: *Let's do it.*

Suddenly we were in the back of a pick-up truck barreling down the road under mossy old oak trees on a steamy Louisiana night. The New Orleans Jazz and Heritage Festival was the day after. The swim was now or never.

Starting around 11:00 pm, the weather broke and the water calmed. With a big frog in my throat, I jumped into the murky waters. We'd gotten underway, but soon realized we could still be in for some trouble. After about an hour and a half of swimming—about three miles in—Capt. Al saw various scattered weather systems on the radar. I felt the chop increase, and we started to get blown into the Causeway bridge. I had to fight against it by swimming to my left, heading diagonally just to keep going straight.

Swimming along, I kept seeing intense flashes. My buddy, Tom Giovagnoli, (Tommy G) was on the boat, and I thought perhaps he had brought along some kind of high tech camera flash. I poked my head up and hollered at the support boat to stop taking pictures because the flashes were freaking me out. Capt. Al informed me that it wasn't a camera. *It was lightning,* and it was all around us.

"Well, should I get in the boat?" I asked.

"You're actually safer in the water!" he shouted back. "The boat is the most dangerous place."

So I put my head down and kept swimming. I chuckled at the sheer absurdity of wondering if my support boat would be struck by lightning. *What then would I do?* I wondered, not chuckling so much anymore—the joke seemed to be on me.

A few hours later in the dark of night with the chop banging me from all directions, I picked up my head to glance at the boat, and it was nowhere in sight.

Gone Pecan.

I was alone. All sorts of thoughts ran through my head. I tried to remain calm by fixing my gaze on the simple green glow stick attached to my leg as if by focusing on it closely enough I could draw the attention of those on the boat. I threw the leg up in the air, circling it around like a water ballet dancer, hoping they would see me. The swells were intense, however, and often I was sunken between them, out of sight if the boat was a ways off. Conversely, the boat's higher profile in the water made it more susceptible to the whims of the wind and the currents.

I'd asked Capt. Al to stay right beside me, but it wasn't so easy with the gusts pushing the boat every which way. At this point, he was pushed so far off, he had to reposition, which meant motoring ahead and turning to the right in a big circle to place himself next to me again. Of course, I only found this out later. At the time, I felt intensely afraid. It was the first time I'd ever felt that way in the water. Here I was, miles offshore in the middle of the lake at night in a storm, seemingly alone. The longer we were apart, the less likely we would be to find each other.

Finally, after what seemed like an eternity (but was probably only a few minutes), the boat shone a light on me.

From then on, we stayed extremely close together, probably too close for a big motor boat, but I was spooked and didn't want to get separated again.

Somehow, after more than seven hours of swimming through the choppiest, most badass water, halfway was in sight. *Oh man!* I thought. *Is it possible we might actually make this?*

Mango never thought I was going to make it, so he wasn't all that concerned about having to swim. Later, I heard that right before we switched, while Mango was trying to get some sleep in the back of the boat on a little mat with a blanket over him, Lenny, my work assistant, who was coordinating logistics, went to relieve himself off the back of the boat and stepped smack dab on Mango's face.

Capt. Allen finally signaled I had made it to the halfway point, and Mango jumped in. We tagged off, and he began the second half. He persevered through bouts of sunshine mixed with violent squalls. I took up position on the little mat in the back of the boat where Mango had received his rude wake-up call. I tried to rest and recover, but it wasn't so easy in a boat being tossed around by the intense weather.

With only a few miles to go and the shore approaching, the Coast Guard pulled up. Turns out, they had issued a Small Craft Advisory on the lake and had come out to check on us. They wanted to see Alan's license and credentials. Meanwhile, Mango pretended not to notice and just kept swimming unsupported towards the lighthouse, which was getting closer by the minute.

He knew full well that soft shell crab po boys, music, family, friends, and the chance to finish this crazy crossing alive were not far away. Rain was pouring down, and we were all in the front of the boat celebrating, dancing, and hollering as we finally came into the harbor of the New Canal Lighthouse. The finish was wet and glorious. Maybe the swim was not all that wise. Maybe we had threaded a needle and tempted fate, but we'd found a way to cross. The weather cleared, and in the following days, Jazz Fest was a celebration of music and life with family and friends. The joy made all the sweeter by the accomplishment.

NO HARM WILL COME TO YOU IN WATER

A lot of planning, preparation, and advance scouting go into these endurance swims. My early swims with Mango laid the groundwork for my solo swim, and prior swims had done the same for the relay swim. Those early swims included some real characters.

Though we didn't know each other then, Coco Robicheaux started his music career playing across the street from my house in Lafayette at Hamilton's Club with his band, The Red Beans and Rice Revue. Coco would go on to become a legendary bluesman and was inducted into the Louisiana Music Hall of Fame. He was a character among characters. At one time, Coco voiced Popeye's Fried Chicken commercials. *Love that chicken from Popeyes!* Through his music he created the mystical world of Spiritland, singing old tales of voodoo and gris-gris from the bayous. Listening to his music feels like being with him in a pirogue under a hoodoo moon skirting through cypress trees.

We will use our voice and hands

To make the music of the Spiritland.

Coco's wife, Danielle Laramie, a singer-songwriter, lives in Nederland, Colorado, up the canyon from Boulder, and Coco would occasionally come up from New Orleans for a spell. He ended up playing a solo gig at my house before a New Orleans Radiators concert at the Fox Theater. I thought he would be an interesting fit for the support boat on one of our first swims on Lake Pontchartrain. I mentioned to him the possibility of coming along.

"Yeah, you rite," he rasped with his signature phrase.

* * * * *

Before our very first swim on Lake Pontchartrain in April, 2009, Mango and I picked up Coco Robicheaux in the old Bywater section of New Orleans at 3:40 am in my friend Allen Blow's old Toyota pickup we called the Mudhauler. Coco had come in from playing music the night before on Frenchman Street. Dressed in sharkskin boots, a leopard print jacket and a decorated black top hat with a chest full of necklaces and trinkets, he didn't exactly look like the boating type. But it was the small Derringer pistol holstered on his hip that caught my eye.

When he noticed me staring, he said, "Just to keep off the bull sharks and the alligators."

Later while swimming, I remember at one point breathing towards the boat to see Coco dipping his cup into the lake—he was using it to make Bloody Marys. I asked him, "Out of Pontchartrain water? Are you crazy?" He said it made the Bloodies nice and salty. I smiled, remembering him taking swigs of Tabasco sauce out of a gigantic bottle before playing at my house. Apparently, it made his voice raspy. About a week after the swim, I received a call from his wife, Danielle, in Alaska, where Coco was on tour. "What happened out on Lake Pontchartrain?" she wanted to know. "He's had the squirts for three days!"

The road was bumpy coming back in the Mudhauler from that swim to the Bywater section of New Orleans. Coco was sitting in the back of the truck on a sack of oyster shells with a Tecate beer in one hand and a soft shell crab po boy in the other. Occasionally, the clutch would pop on the old truck or we'd hit a pothole, and he'd get thrown and his beer would splash.

"*Hey Now..!*" he'd holler.

As we dropped him off back in the Bywater, he climbed out of the back and we gave each other a big hug. Before he turned to go, I said, "Hey Coco, do you have a blessing for us?"

He looked at me quizzically, "Man, you don't need no blessing. You're already blessed."

He was right. I felt foolish even for asking.

That would be the last time I saw him. He was one of those characters who mysteriously appeared in my life at different times and places. From across my house in Lafayette to Lake Pontchartrain to Boulder and points in between. Once at Burning Man, I spotted in the distance this art car on the playa that looked like a huge New Orleans paddlewheel boat. On one of my first nights in the vast Black Rock desert of Nevada, I walked up to the gated entrance of the huge boat with fire blasting out of the smokestacks on top and music pounding on the fiesta deck above, and I heard the unmistakably seasoned voice. "Welcome aboard, M&M!"

There was Coco, hoodoo doctor, bayou shaman, freaking doorman and greeter on the *Lady Sassafras*. Out in the middle of nowhere in the Black Rock Desert. As I came aboard, he draped one arm over my shoulder, his other arm sweeping over the pulsating sand as he leaned close and whispered, "Burning Man is like walking around in your dreams."

The year he passed away, 2011, Danielle sent along to Burning Man a care package for a few of Coco's friends. Among the gifts was a patterned Balinese vest with my name on it. In the pocket was a piece of round bone about the size of a wooden nickel. Coco had carved intricate hoodoo symbols on one side.

On the other he had carved, *No harm will come to you in water.*

Coco Robicheaux drinking a Bloody Mary on Lake Pontchartrain

FOLLOW THE MERMAID

After all the adventures through the years, I was no stranger to the challenges of Lake Pontchartrain. And yet, on the solo swim crossing I was alone.

Those early boondoggles with Mango were not only the formative years of exploring open water long distance swimming, they were also some of the best times I've ever had. But at this point in my life—after the leg injury—I was looking for something more. It was time to grow and to put myself to a new test. It had been a comfort to pass the baton to Mango at the halfway point. Now I needed to go the full distance myself. And for that, I had to pull all I needed from somewhere within.

I had been in the choppy brackish water of Lake Pontchartrain for over twelve hours now. I had pushed through the harshness of sunrise, but serious fatigue was setting in. The small wind from the northeast had required that I adjust my stroke, and now it was difficult to make a full rotation with my left shoulder. Things were getting especially serious after feedings. I would feel like I needed to pass gas, and the nutrients I had just consumed would all come running out. Concerned, Kristin had taken up position on the bow of the boat with her legs swinging overboard and her eyes fixed on me. Seeing her there perched on the boat, looking stylish with a captain's hat, provided some measure of comfort every time I breathed to my left.

While I could see the shore in the far-off distance, it didn't seem to be getting any closer. Delirium began to take hold as I started questioning everything. *Had external forces conspired against me? Had I lost all powers of locomotion*? Or was I just going *loco*?

I remembered something: Coco's talisman. To me, the engraving is a ticket for safe passage. I repeat the phrase when I become afraid. When I'm standing on the edge of an abyss at midnight and my heart feels like it's going to explode. When I want to run back to bed and curl up under the covers. When headwinds whip up, I repeat the phrase. Over the years, it has become not just a mantra, but a life philosophy.

No harm will come to you in water.

Coco Robicheaux had sent a blessing, after all.

I kept repeating it even as I stroked toward a destination that seemed to recede faster than I could swim.

After several more hours, I could sense a little more excitement on the boat. A little more hooting and hollering as time progressed. My shoulders burned as if they were slow cooking on a rotisserie over hot coals. Around and around again.

Then I saw the entrance to the bay and beyond that, a glimpse of the boat ramp of the finish. Allen Blow shouted to me, "Follow the Mermaid!" The figure on top of his boat had pointed the way for the entire swim, and now it would lead me to the final destination. I wondered if Lord Byron's soul had managed to transmigrate back into a merman after all.

"Follow the mermaid!" Allen Blow shouted several more times. Okay, so maybe it was a *merman*, but the distinction was irrelevant. With what lucidity was left, I thought of all the work and the training and the people who were on the support boats and our journeys together. And, of course, there was Lady K, my biggest fan, cheering me on. Her look of concern was now all smiles.

Now that I knew for sure the finish was within grasp, my shoulders and back started heaving from all the emotion. Tension, fear, and pain were released. And into that place rushed joy. It came bubbling forth from somewhere deep in my belly. I stopped for a second, and Randy asked if I was alright. All I could do was look at him. I couldn't put the totality of the experience into words. But I don't think it needed an explanation. His look said he already knew. *You did it, Mateo.*

I would only find out later, that while I was overcome with

all those feelings, an alligator was sunning itself on the very boat ramp where I was to finish. That might explain the fire trucks, ambulances, and all manner of first responders. Turns out a few Cajun fishermen hooked the alligator and caught it. The next day on the front page of the *Times Picayune*, the headline read, "Alligator pulled from the lake in Mandeville as swimmer nears." Curtis Robinson, our official observer, conjectured that the public information officer at the city likely received an interesting call. *"We've got a situation... An open water swimmer is approaching on a record-breaking swim. We've got national media. And an alligator."*

Alligator pulled from Lake Pontchartrain

As we closed in, I could start to make out the crowd on the boat dock. It was bigger than I'd expected. (Maybe it was the alligator?) I could see camera crews and well-wishers. All floating and surreal. I had visualized this finish so many times, and here it was, a reality rising up to greet me.

Finally, my fingers ran through muck and mud, then scraped the slimy cement of the boat ramp. One final challenge remained: to get through the thick green algae lining the shore for several feet. Hopefully, there wasn't another alligator lurking underneath. *Save the best for last, eh?*

Standing up, I heard a big roar from the crowd of several hundred. The mayor of Mandeville wanted to greet me with a big hug while I was still in the water, but technically this could have compromised the swim according to the rules and disqualified me. Coach Randy pushed him aside and told him not to touch me until I had cleared the water.

After swimming 24.6 miles in 14 hours and 56 minutes, I stepped onto terra firma, threw my hands in the air, and let out a primal yell. All my support team and family circled around. Someone gave me a bottle of champagne. The evening news carried the clip of me with Kristin's arm draped over my shoulder. After taking a big splashy swig, I hollered, "We made history today!"

* * * * *

But in New Orleans there is always more history layered beneath more history. Later, I received a call from a *Times Picayune* reporter about one Ernest C. Hunt. There wasn't much about the particulars of his swim, but yellowed records clearly stated that he had crossed the lake in 1923. Had Hunt crawled out of the dusty archive to snatch my record and claim his rightful place in history? I admit that at first I was a little disappointed. But when I took a closer look, some key differences emerged. Hunt had swum in a different direction, going north shore to south. Moreover, his swim was 22 miles, not 24.6. There also wasn't any indication he'd followed the same rules. But, whatever. More important were the similarities between our swims. Hunt had swum across the lake and through the night. He was a kindred spirit. A soul brother. The only other person in the world who shared what I went through.

After contemplating it all for a while, I recognized that being 'the first' is not why I swim. While I understand why making history is appealing and of such significance to the Marathon Swimmers Federation and the World Open Water Swimming Association, it's not the most important factor for me. There is also a certain trickiness in claiming to be the "first" in anything—or the fastest. On just about any popular hiking trail or point-to-point sailing adventure point, FKTs (Fastest Known Times) have become very popular of late. There are records and FKTs for hangliding, climbing, cross-country skiing, hot-air ballooning, rowing—you name it. History is a strange bedfellow. You never know what might have occurred in the past, who might have done what in record-setting fashion.

Finding out about Ernest Hunt's swim 90 years prior, I was initially a little disheartened. But far from being disappointed, I was honored to follow in Hunt's wake.

* * * * *

I remember after the swim on Lake Pontchartrain, it took nearly two days for my appetite to return, but once it did, it came roaring back with a vengeance. Despite being exhausted, I had trouble sleeping. All the adrenaline and pushing my body to extremes had thrown me off. My shoulders felt as though a cinder block was tied to the top of each.

My first job out of college was working at one of the top restaurants in America, Commander's Palace with chef Emeril Lagasse. Two days after the swim, we had a party of twelve in the upstairs Garden Room, which is cradled in the branches of a magnificent 200-year-old oak tree. Curtis Robinson always likes to say that while I'm a pretty good swimmer, my real talent is Endurance Lunching.

Later that evening Allen and Jennifer Blow threw a big crawfish boil, and Papa Mali and David Amram played in their living room. Outside was a grocery cart fashioned into a raging bull of a roving musical DJ cart. There was a generator, lights, speakers, a mixing board, and laptop station. The creator and operator of this unique contraption was none other than Captain Michael Feduccia. That was the first time we met, and it led to him becoming the boat captain on one of the Caribbean swims.

When I look back at all the transformative moments of my life, with the exception of getting married and having children, I consider swimming Lake Pontchartrain a pinnacle moment. As Lord Byron did his Hellespont swim. For me, it was the culmination of years of scoping and planning. A celebration of water and New Orleans. A dream-like circus concocted out of thin air. Plus, it was a comeback. The leg injury had brought on a long period of pain, loneliness, and emotional struggle, but coming out of it, I still managed to forge something greater than I had done before. There was a particular irony: Through the experience of shattering my leg, I became stronger and more whole than I'd ever been.

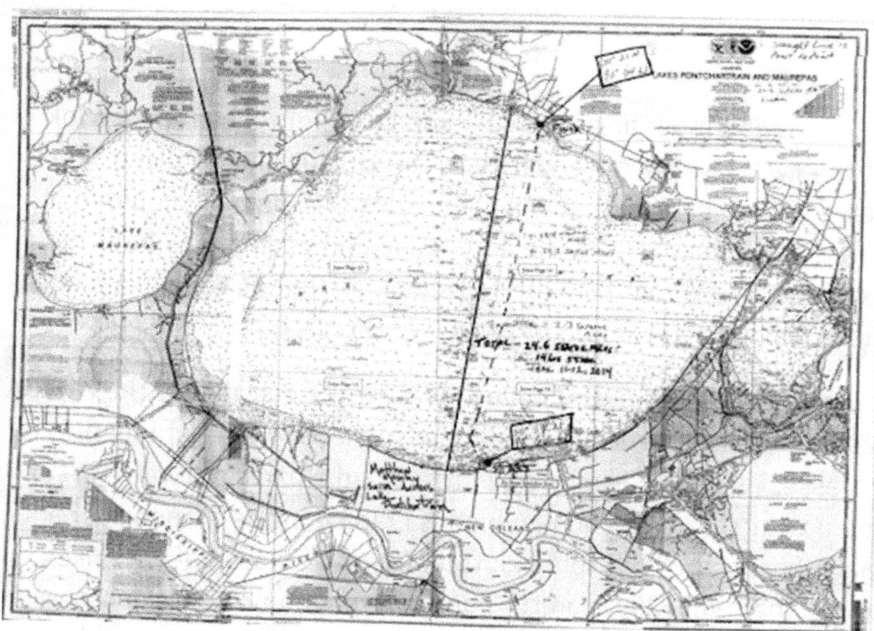

Map of Lake Pontchartrain Swim

Moseley emerges after swimming Pontchartrain

David Amram playing jazz through the night

Coco Robicheaux

CHAPTER SIX
SWIMMING THE CARIBBEAN

THE GREAT BLUE RIVER

I was standing on the shores of Playa Tamarindo under the stars on the island of Culebra, looking west toward Fajardo, Puerto Rico, about 20 miles away. Normally if I was on the beach at 3:00 a.m., I'd be dancing with friends, drink in hand. This time I was about to swim across the dark abyss between the islands.

Over the years, Randy Soler had taken me to Puerto Rico and the Caribbean for several training swims. We'd visited various beaches and islands, including Culebra, at the easternmost edge of the U.S. Virgin Islands. It was during one of those trips that Randy cooked up the notion of this swim in his home waters. He'd planned all the complicated logistics. This time, I'd be swimming for the Scuba Dogs Society, which protects and cleans coral reefs.

Standing there on that beautiful beach on that enchanted night, we had just one problem. There was a misunderstanding about our location. Captain Rony, on a boat called the Reef Sniper, was having trouble finding us because Playa Tamarindo is rather secluded. I waited for nearly 30 minutes with zinc oxide covering my body and my goggles at the ready, just focused on staying calm before Captain Rony finally arrived. With a nearly full moon hanging low on the horizon, I waded into gentle waters. (Yes, I like timing these swims around a full moon.)

It was 3:40 a.m. When we passed the first little island of Cayo Luis Peña a mile out, the glow from the blue and green lights on Randy's kayak illuminated the bottom, and I could see fish. I wondered if the 15-foot hammerhead sharks known to inhabit the bay knew I was there.

As we moved into deeper waters just before sunrise, I started noticing bioluminescence following the swoosh of my strokes. I imagined the electrical impulses of light as tiny aquatic angels sending me off, the spirits of the ocean wishing me well on my journey. I relaxed. All the nervous energy of the delayed start began to fade as a smooth and easy stroke took hold.

Swimming at night evokes a certain timelessness. Under the rising moon, the simple act of being alive and kicking brought a smile. No clock. No race. Everything stripped to its fundamentals. I felt a deep communion with the water and the moon. It was just my paddler and those blue and green LED lights. In this way, swimming at night feels like transcending both time and space.

As the sun rose behind me in the east, we were three miles into the swim and feeling the joy that accompanies most travelers when they start out on a journey. To be sure, we knew there could be dragons to slay later, but for the time being, we were all together and moving across the water as a unit. Pedro Umpierre was leading the way, directing Captain Rony. The *Reef Sniper* was a big boat and, as during the Lake Pontchartrain swim, there was a band, Los Boppers, playing live music at sunrise. I could sometimes hear the steady *thawp* of their latin congas.

As we continued to move northwest past the little *cayos*, Pedro pointed out the last two islands on our left that marked the beginning of the Caribbean Sea. We were entering the Gulf Stream, which pushes north to the middle of the Atlantic. There was some disagreement with Captain Rony over the course because getting up to the Gulf Stream took us two miles off the most direct route. Pedro insisted it would be faster. I had hoped these kinds of questions had been worked out beforehand. But I trusted Pedro, an expert sailor and boatman I met through my previous training swims in Puerto Rico. He was also a triathlete and had competed in the World Championships. I figured he knew what he was talking about.

An hour later as I swam past the final little *cayo*, I could feel a distinct change in the current. This stretch of water has become nearly mythical in the literary imagination. A couple of years before composing *The Old Man and the Sea*, Ernest Hemingway wrote an article for the July 1949 edition of *Holiday* magazine titled after his nickname for the Gulf Stream, "The Great Blue River." He writes, "People ask you why you live in Cuba and you say it is because you like it... you tell them the biggest reason you live in Cuba is the great, deep blue river, three quarters of a mile to a mile deep and sixty to eighty miles across... When the Gulf Stream is running well, it is a dark blue and there are whirlpools along the edges."

Now that I was in "the great blue river" of the Gulf Stream, swells and giant rollers were coming in at very predictable intervals pushing me along at three and a half miles per hour. I was locked into a steady cadence: two strokes right, two left. Three strokes right looking at Randy, three strokes left looking at Pedro and the *Reef Sniper*. Five strokes, breathe right. Five strokes, breathe left. Repeat the whole cycle. Kicking to the beat with my head down. Swimming from the belly and the core of my body while my shoulders stay relaxed. After training at high altitudes in Colorado, swimming at sea level and with the added buoyancy of salt water, you feel like you have a boost in oxygen and flotation.

Obsessively tracking time is not my style. I keep a general sense of where I am, however. Judging by my regular feedings of electrolytes, eggs, gels, and lots of water every 20 to 25 minutes, I figured we were about halfway, and I was fine with the ballpark estimate. I just needed to keep swimming until it was over. After all, I'd tell myself, fish don't tell time.

Fish seem fairly unemotional to me, especially about swimming. They just do it. Like humans walk on land. When I'm swimming, I try to channel the energy of a fish and can even convince myself I consist of scales, fins, and gills. I'm not sure if this is an acknowledged practice by sports psychologists, but it seems to work for me.

At that point, I was feeling powerful with each stroke. For many hours in the daytime, I was swimming through a blue orb of light streaming up from the bottom of the ocean. It was the reflection of the sun through the water, and it looked as if the sun were sitting on the ocean floor instead of in the sky. The light encircled our crew like a shield of golden energy. In reality, protection came from an eight-foot-long black cord on Randy's kayak that emitted an electrical signal to keep away sharks. There hadn't been any reported shark-human interactions in the area, but it gave me peace of mind, nevertheless.

Well, there was one moment of terror. Through the water I saw a small black figure in the depths. Suddenly, it shot up right at me. The streak from nowhere freaked me out.

Right before it got to me, I realized it was Captain Rony, who's a free diver. He had gone ahead and jumped off with his flippers. He recorded some great deep underwater footage of me swimming, but it scared the *caca* out of me. Everyone on the boat had a good laugh.

Just keep swimming, I thought as usual. Miles later, passing Cayo Palomino, we turned slightly south and said goodbye to the great blue river and the pulsing rollers that had pushed me toward Puerto Rico. The outline of hotels and beaches in Fajardo started to appear.

At this point, Randy and I had trained together for several years. We had been through the fire and back again on Lake Pontchartrain. Many of his friends and family had gathered on the shore. I could see him getting emotional, wiping away tears behind his sunglasses. I figured his emotions matched my own. Overwhelming joy. Gratitude for being alive and able to cross this sea.

I gave him the universal *shaka* wave with my thumb and pinky sticking out, a little signal I knew what he was feeling. In the water, the Hawaiian sign was the only way to express friendship, gratitude, unity, but most of all encouragement. *We are in this together.*

Sometimes all your suffering lets you know your joy. I

thought of our children. I was so happy that Kristin, who was waiting for me at the finish, had flown through the night from Colorado to meet me with my wedding ring (I hadn't worn it because I was afraid it would fall off in the water). I had lived many a Hero's Journey, and I was about to finish another chapter. Waves of emotion rolled up my spine. Randy and I never said a word to each other—not even afterward. We didn't need to. That moment was the highlight of the swim. It was all I needed to answer the most important question of all, *Why*? Right then, the swim as a whole became greater than the sum of its parts.

Unfortunately, there were more parts to come. By my calculations, with the boost from the Gulf Stream, I would be done in under three hours. In this instance, I must plead guilty to faulty expectation management. After the magic of the moment, the shore didn't get any closer. Time seemed to stand still, and it dawned on me we may have celebrated too soon. What I thought was going to be two hours to finish turned into another six hours of fighting an outgoing tide. A palm tree on a small *cayo* just wouldn't budge. For about half an hour, a foot-long fish that looked very similar to Nemo swam with me out in front of Randy's boat. As if guiding the way. At one point, the little fish turned under the kayak and swam back to his abode on the coral reef we had crossed a little ways back. As I turned my head to watch it swim away, I ran straight into Randy's kayak and cracked my head hard. I touched my head to check for blood.

"What happened?" Randy shouted.

I didn't even bother to explain. *Pay attention and pull yourself together*, I thought. I put my head down and kept swimming.

Randy had warned me about the seaweed and the thick grasses at the boat ramp at the finish. Swimming into it all, I could barely move my arms. The viscous slimy mass smelled so bad I dry-heaved and nearly vomited. But I couldn't care less. I had just completed the first-known swim from Culebra to Fajardo. Thirty-eight kilometers (almost 24 miles) in 12 hours, 1 minute, and 55 seconds.

Hugging Randy Soler after swimming from Culebra to Farjardo

We slept and rested the entire next day back at our compound at the Zoni Beach House in Culebra. We lay by the pool, drinking mimosas for breakfast and spent the afternoon at Playa Flamenco, widely considered one the most beautiful beaches in the world. These are some of the fringe benefits of long distance swimming around Puerto Rico.

Two days after the swim, the whole team and other friends came back to the Zoni Beach House for a dinner and celebration. Well after midnight, we all went to Playa Tamarindo, the beach where we had started the swim. While we swam naked in the ocean under the moon, the angels who had greeted me at the start of the swim, returned. Bioluminescent spirits glowed all around us as we splashed about. They had come to celebrate with us.

GOAL INFLATION

After many swims around the azure waters and visits to their beautiful island over the years, I reserve a special place in my heart for the people of Puerto Rico. They remind me of New Orleanians: soulful, resilient, and wild about live music and dancing. Puerto Ricans invented salsa. They are boisterous, endlessly entertaining storytellers. They are stylish and dress up to go out on the town. With music spilling out of open doorways and secret alleys, Old San Juan suggests what New Orleans would be like if it were on the ocean.

After a big team dinner, a storm moved through Culebra and knocked out power at the Zoni Beach House. We swam in the pool and talked by candlelight deep into the night. When Pedro Umpierre shone a light on an old and dated map of the Caribbean in the corner of the kitchen, Randy and I gathered around. We started scheming about other possible swims. *What about this to that? What about here to there?* Starting points, ending points. We laughed in the afterglow of our swim. That night with the power out and just candles and a flashlight, having successfully done the Culebra-to-Fajardo swim, Randy and I set our sights on something bigger.

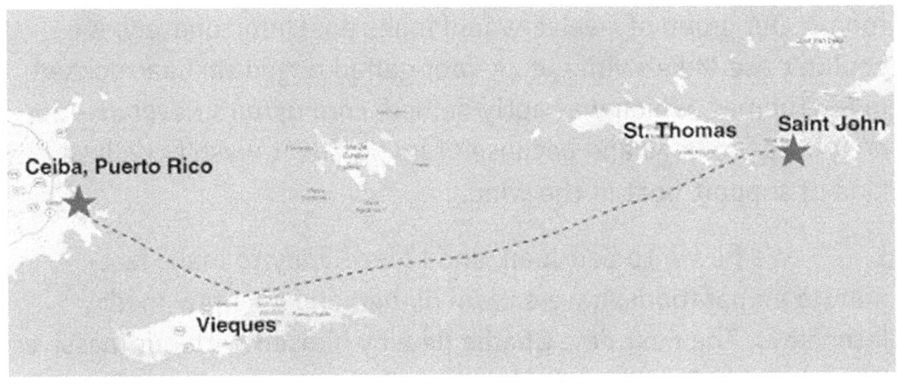

St. John to St. Thomas, to Vieques, to Puerto Rico

The Culebra-to-Fajardo swim was glorious. Naturally, we had to do more. In 2017, after a year of planning with Randy—and a lot more training—we set for ourselves the massive task of swimming a part of the Caribbean in three legs: St. John to St. Thomas. St. Thomas to Vieques. Then Vieques to Puerto Rico.

In addition to teaming up with the Scuba Dogs Society again, we were joined by two others. Carolynn Box is a scientist who studies plastics in water and serves as environmental coordinator for 5 Gyres Institute, which works to combat plastic pollution. Vicki Nicholas Goldstein is the founder and executive director of the Inland Ocean Coalition, an environmental organization for which I was on the board of directors. Thankfully, Pedro Umpierre returned, this time bringing his lovely wife, Rose. In my time in the Caribbean he'd become a good friend and let me post up at his condo in the Caribe Hilton on the ocean in San Juan. A solid, calming influence on these Caribbean swims, Pedro brought a lot to the team, and I trusted his knowledge. Randy was my coach, but Pedro was our guide.

My son, Charlie, who had just turned 14, joined the adventure. The trip was a Christmas gift, though at certain points he probably questioned whether the gift was actually a curse. Michael Feduccia, my friend from New Orleans, who was living in the Virgin Islands chartering sailboats, was enlisted as the captain of a 42-foot catamaran, which slept eight comfortably in its four rooms. Our group of twelve would make do. Unfortunately, we couldn't use Mike's vintage 45-foot gaffed rigged sailboat docked in St. Thomas, which was aptly named, *Lord Byron's Revenge*—our crew was too large and because of its profile, it wasn't the best kind of support boat in the wind.

We flew into San Juan, and I met Randy to make last-minute preparations, have a team dinner, and do a few media interviews. The next day, Charlie flew by himself with our massive 80-gallon RovR cooler—RovR is one of my sponsors—to meet Capt. Mike, pick up the boat in Tortola, and get food and rations.

We started at 3:00 a.m. with the winds whipping up furious chop. Mark Williams was by my side in the kayak with John Mans filming from the boat. Just putting the kayak in the water off the catamaran and getting Mark into it proved a challenge. When I jumped in, terror shot through me. Attached beneath the kayak was a device that repelled sharks by emitting electrical pulses, but it certainly didn't help with the choppy waters.

"Most people boating at night in the North Caribbean sea are not out there doing something safe," recalled Captain Mike years later. "In the Caribbean, there are shoals, rocks, and reefs that can send nearly any vessel to its demise, some of which are not even marked on the chart." He said that hopefully by sunset the boat is tied to a mooring ball and you're preparing a nice dinner, not out on the high seas with a swimmer on your starboard side.

As I swam through the dark, the sailboat kept moving all around. One minute it was behind me, then ahead of me, then on my left going backward. My frustration, linked directly to my fear, spiked whenever Mark and I found ourselves alone on the open ocean. As on Lake Pontchartrain, one of the big challenges with the wind was the difference in profiles among the seacraft. The large sailboat, so much taller than us, was much more susceptible to the gales. Capt. Mike was constantly forced to do giant circles around us to keep us together. Otherwise, the boat would be blown away from us, which happened several times. The experience was similar to when I was lost in the dark on Lake Pontchartrain. Mike Feduccia thereafter became known as Captain Perfect Circles.

Carolynn Box, the scientist, conducted research on the plastic content of the water. She trailed a large sieve-like device behind the boat to collect debris while I swam. The institute would bottle up samples of debris and analyze them for microplastics. Carolynn discovered that even if the sea was relatively clear, the islands of the Caribbean acted as a giant colander where certain beaches caught the lion's share of debris.

For years, 5 Gyres has been sounding the alarm about polyfluoroalkyl substances (PFAS), plastics considered 'forever chemicals' because they don't break down over time. They are used in stain repellents and coatings and are found in carpets, furniture, clothing, food packaging, and innumerable other consumer products. PFAS are the enemy of water molecules because they can stick to them and have been found in waterways everywhere around the planet, including the most unlikely of places—the Arctic Ocean. As such, they contaminate the global seafood supply. PFAS are linked to devastating health impacts such as cancer, liver damage, thyroid problems, and asthma. These forever chemicals have been detected in all major U.S. water supplies, which means we are literally drinking plastic. Teaming up with me, Carolyn Box, 5 Gyres, and the Inland Ocean Coalition would advance this important work.

* * * * *

Occasionally seaweed or debris, and sometimes the jetsam of plastic bottles or bags would pass underneath, giving me the feeling of charging towards Vieques. At times wildlife—fish, turtles, even manatees—would swim by. But I have to admit, after a while, I was mostly motivated by what awaited us following the swim to Vieques. The W Hotel was giving us a few rooms and organizing a champagne reception with the mayor of the island and the Boys and Girls Club of Vieques.

From the conversations I picked up on the radio between feedings, I gathered that tensions were running high on the boat. Randy had broken his arm a few weeks before and wasn't able to be next to me in the kayak accompanying Mark. Perhaps because of the distance from me, Randy had a lot of nervous energy, and it was impacting others on the boat. Mike had to remind him at one point that he was the one listed as the captain of the boat and that he alone would be making the navigation decisions. At feedings, Mark would turn off the radio to stop Randy from bombarding us with orders and instructions.

Having paddled for me in all sorts of situations, Mark has never, ever complained or faltered. This time, he held formation and position flawlessly. When I sneak a breath on my dominant right side, I like to see the nose of the kayak under my rotating arm, and that's where Mark always was. I would find out only later that Mark was puking from seasickness on the other side of the kayak so I wouldn't see. He had never been seasick in his life and was an expert boatman, but the choppy waters got to him this time.

Mark was working hard. His seasickness was indicative of just how rough the waters were. At some points, he struggled to keep upright as five- and six-foot swells would sweep by, threatening to capsize the kayak.

Often on swims, there are periods of bliss, zen-like peace of mind, feeling utterly free in the water. When I swim with bioluminescent creatures, it's like entering a dream state and being overwhelmed by euphoria. Not this time. There was never a moment when I could just relax and have fun. Swimming required constant vigilance to avoid inhaling the ocean water when a wave smacked me in the face. It demanded I stay focused, kicking, and keeping my butt up to avoid sinking into the chop. It was critical I stay right next to Mark.

The day passed by, and the stretch of water never seemed to end. I summoned every mental conditioning technique I could—all my strength and training. As I look back now, swimming the Caribbean was likely the most difficult swim of my life in many ways, such as fighting current and wind. I could never just relax and take simple pleasure in being in the water. I had to reach deep.

My relationship with my son Charlie is one of the great treasures in my life. We've gone to the New Orleans Jazz and Heritage Festival together, a bunch of music shows, and have shared a lot of experiences on the water and river trips. I was overjoyed to have him on this Caribbean swim. As we got closer to the finish, one thought above all fueled me: embracing Charlie once I reached shore. I wanted to give him a big hug and not let go. We had become very close over the last year; I watched him grow up on this trip. Capt. Mike had christened Charlie "Fresh Mate," and he became Mike's helper, friend, and occasional bartender.

Those last few miles were as painful as any I'd ever swum. Torturous. My lower back was burned to a crisp, lips and tongue swollen from the salty water, underarms and the nape of my neck chafed raw. I was starving and dehydrated.

Finally, the moment arrived.

Mark guided me into a beautiful little beach where I could see the whole team. I crawled from the water onto the welcoming sand before getting my legs under me and stumbling the next ten feet to the shore. The boat horn blew along with *hoots* and *hollahs* from the team.

Charlie came out a few yards to meet me and swam in with me, careful not to touch me until I had cleared the water. After tumbling from the shallow water with wobbly legs, I stood up on the shore. Once again, I threw my arms over my head in elation. Then I hugged Charlie and held him tight. It was a father-and-son moment I revisit often.

Hugging Charles Moseley on Culebrita

Only then did I realize something was amiss. *Where was the W Hotel with the champagne reception? Where was the mayor and the Boys and Girls Club?* I wondered. *Where was the cabana where I could lie down and take a breather?* After all the hugs and high fives, Randy gave me the news: we weren't on Vieques, after all. We'd been blown westward over 20 miles off course and were now standing on the little island of Culebrita.

In a twist of irony, we were about a kilometer away from the island where I had begun my first swim the year before for the Culebra-to-Fajardo swim. I swam 24.5 miles from St. Thomas to Culebrita in just over 15 hours.

* * * * *

Later, I would learn there had been a lot of discussion among Capt. Mike, Randy, and Pedro (and radioing to Mark on the kayak) about our direction and progress. Throughout the swim, Randy thought we were making headway, but Capt. Mike knew there were problems. He'd been doing calculations throughout the day. All of them showed we were not moving to Vieques to the south, but being pushed hard to the west.

Captain Mike recalled later that as I swam outside from St. Thomas after several miles, there was a monolith of a rock formation that wouldn't move. Because Captain Mike had the rock for a reference, he knew we were stuck in a current without any forward trajectory. While it felt like we were moving, the monolithic rock told a different story.

Friction ensued. Capt. Mike told Randy something like, "I don't argue with GPS devices and tape measures." They had debated about telling me the current was pulling me away from Vieques, but decided against it in the end. They figured if they told me, I'd have stopped swimming and gotten in the boat. They would have been right. Instead, they let me keep swimming until we came upon the first island of Culebrita. Amanda McCracken wrote in *Men's Journal* about the disagreement, "Moseley's 15-year-old son, Charlie, concurred, 'Dad is going to be pissed if we show up on an island other than Vieques.' Captain Feduccia's handlebar mustache turned up into a smile as he responded to Charlie: 'You'll find that in life you think you are going the wrong direction and instead find it to be the right place.'"

* * * * *

A few days later, sitting at the swim-up bar at the Caribe Hilton in San Juan, Puerto Rico, on the way back to Boulder, Charlie and I had a good laugh at the whole blasted and burnt adventure. With everything that had happened, with all the planning and putting together a seasoned team, and the sheer enormity of it all, I came to realize that sometimes in life you end up on the wrong island.

Expect the unexpected.

CHAPTER SEVEN

GARDEN OF ROCKS

"Rivers are like people. We never destroy a river, for to do so would be to destroy ourselves."

– Wade Davis, "Magdalena, River of Dreams"

By 1:45 p.m., over eight hours in the water, my stroke through the Green River is feeling strong and powerful. Sinking into the experience, I'm wide awake and in control. Perhaps I'm absorbing the vibes around me. Every third stroke, I take a breath and can pick up the team's chatter. I can't make out the words, but the tone is clear. I can tell when they're laughing, which is about half the time. At the next feeding, I'll ask what had cracked them up and hear some wild anecdote, like the one about an Alaskan friend who worked for Greenpeace and crashed his boat into a whaler.

There's a feedback loop between the team and me. When they're feeling lighthearted, I feel extra buoyant. As on most big swims, when I'm struggling with aches and pains, the chatter of the team trails off and their facial expressions turn dour.

It's that part of the day when the sun is content to settle into its perch above, and it feels like the present will extend indefinitely. All too easy to forget about minutes, if not hours. As I noted, while I try not to get wrapped up in the time I'm making, I usually have a sense of how many feedings I've completed. By such simple metrics, I figure we're coming up to a section where the river narrows and I'll have to tuck my legs to stand and walk across a gravel bar.

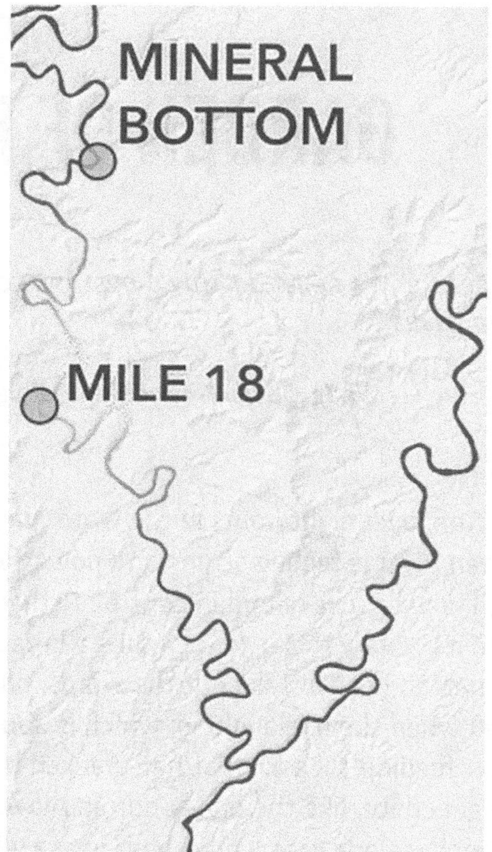

Mineral Bottom to Mile 18

As expected, when we round the bend at the 18-mile mark, we hear the hiss and rumble of the stony shallows. I grab my Chaco sandals hanging from a carabiner at the front of Mark's kayak. Where the water pours into a rivulet on river right it's just deep enough for the kayaks and the canoe to skate across, but not for me. As I pull on my sandals I collide with the rocks just under the surface. I hit with my hip and roll against the rocks with the current, all while slipping on my second sandal.

As soon as it's on, I pop to my feet. The rocks are slick and covered with algae. With the water rushing through, they can be tricky to navigate. A foot can get wedged all too easily, snapping an ankle. Even a slip and fall may bring the whole swim to an abrupt end, sending me back to the Moab hospital.

You might wonder if walking across the rocks broke WOWSA rules. Well, I'd worried about the same thing and had to check. It turns out, there is an official allowance for shallow water. Rule 7.17 states, "Athletes, if they encounter a shallow area along the course (e.g., within a coral reef, on a sandbar, along a jetty, or near a pier), may stand up if allowed by the Referee or Safety Officer for safety reasons. However, they may not walk along the course, dolphin or jump in the forward motion to gain an advantage."

I'm sure not walking across those slippery rocks to gain an advantage. To be perfectly clear, getting up out of the water and exposing myself to the air actually constitutes a distinct disadvantage. It lowers my body temperature and adds to my fatigue. Standing up and walking requires much more energy than swimming and is much slower. If it can be avoided at all, it should be.

My Green River expedition isn't the first to run aground. Within a mile of launching, one of Powell's boats hit a sandbar in the middle of the water. The crew figured the boat was overloaded and that deer and bighorn sheep could be hunted for food later, so they jettisoned most of their 500 pounds of bacon. It was a decision they came to regret during the second half of their trip, when both food and quarry dwindled.

We are far more fortunate. On the beach at the far end of the rock garden, I scarf down some leftover chicken lettuce wraps from the team dinner the night before. They must be the culinary opposite of what Powell's men were subjected to. The handfuls I shove into my mouth taste delicious. The team resupplies water bottles from the larger jugs, and I'm back swimming.

BORN TO SWIM

While crawling across the shallow rivers and sandbars and rolling up onto rock gardens might be annoying for me, the act is rooted in prehistory. In 2006, scientists announced the discovery of a 375-million-year-old fossil, a "fishapod," in the Canadian Arctic. As the specimen has traits of both an amphibian and a fish, its discovery points to one of the most pivotal junctures in the evolutionary history of the animal kingdom: the moment when fish ventured out of the water and onto land. Which means that atavistically man is a fish out of water.

Dr. Neil Shubin, author of *Your Inner Fish*, and his colleagues named the fossil *Tiktaalik roseae*. Tiktaalik is an Inuit word for 'burbot,' a cod-like fish. Dr. Shubin and his fellow scientists call it a "transitional fossil," and they think it possessed both gills and rudimentary lungs. It is also the earliest known fish with a neck. Not quite a 'walking fish,' but close.

Shubin and a team of paleontologists hypothesized that Tiktaalik had evolved to be able to thrive in swampy habitats and shallow marshy stream systems. Confluences and sand bars. The point being, Tiktaalik was developing into a creature that could transition onto the land—a hugely significant development in our evolutionary biology.

In his book, Dr. Shubin chronicles this evolution. He explains how terrestrial animals arose over the course of millions of years. Wrist bones evolved to supplement their fins, which granted them the ability to prop themselves up and drag themselves. Eventually, they could crawl out of the water in search of food or to get away from predators. Over time, these fins with wrist bones evolved into arms and the tail separated to form legs. The real evolutionary jump came with lungs that allowed for the breathing of air.

On long distance swims, and especially when walking across sandbars, I think of Tiktaalik as one of my avatars. When I'm in the water for an extended period, my body adapts as if I'm regressing to a transitional state. My fingernails grow noticeably faster and my skin becomes scaly. My neck stays elongated, breathing, sighting, searching around. The tongue swells. After all these years, I'm still waiting to see if a turtle-like shell starts to develop on my back, which is already weathered and leathered.

On occasion, I feel like a dolphin, a species that returned to water after having evolved into a mammal on land.

Recent trends seem to be headed in the opposite direction, however, prompting more terrestrialization, not less. In *Life's Matrix: A Biography of Water*, author Philip Ball reminds us that "until comparatively recently, an aquatic environment was the sole milieu for life on Earth. The planet has apparently hosted living organisms for an astonishing 3.8 billion years of its 4.6-billion-year history, and yet colonization of the land began only around 450 million years ago."

* * * * *

When Fiebig announces we're at mile 28, I'm taken aback. Given the regular feedings, I'm sure I've swum over 31 miles. A slight disagreement ensues. He finally says something like, "Dude, I'm the guy with the map. I know where we are." He's right, of course. I'm just disappointed because we are slightly off the pace. This is a reminder of why I don't like to ask where I am. The three-mile difference means we are now an hour behind schedule.

I put my head down and keep swimming, determined not to let the news dispirit me any more than it already has. My optimism's already taken a hit. After running into the gravel bar earlier, I haven't been able to get over the low flows. I guess it's mind over matter: I keep sensing the river's sluggishness. The added *oomph* the current gave me earlier seems to have diminished. It feels as if the moving walkway beneath my feet has slowed down, giving less and demanding more. Whether that sensation is just in my head or not, I imagine the drop in CFS (cubic feet per second, the standard measurement of volume and speed of water) accounts for the three-mile discrepancy.

So, what does it mean for the game plan? After a quick recalculation, we determine I've fallen off the scheduled 3 m.p.h. rate. I'll have to make up time by speeding up. It's just gonna have to be a comeback, I think to myself. That's alright. I'm no stranger to comebacks.

* * * * *

When it comes to Western water, *aridification* is accelerating with alarming rapidity. The Colorado River doesn't even reach the Gulf of California anymore. As water levels plunge, Lake Powell and Lake Mead are showing more and more bathtub rings (and more corpses!). Running into the sandbar only recalled news I'd heard the day before, news I'd been trying to ignore as if by pushing it out of my mind I could somehow negate it altogether.

Bego Gerhart, a legendary old-school park ranger in Canyonlands, had stopped by our campsite at Mineral Bottom for an afternoon chat before we put in. He is friends with Fiebig and had accompanied him and Jenny on their Source to Sea trip when they rafted through Cataract Canyon. Ranger Bego gave us the sobering news that the Green River's water flow was at 1,800 CFS.

The lowest flows ever recorded for that time of year.

The river was eight times lower than it should be. Running into rocks and sandbars, scraping the bottom on so many strokes that my knuckles were raw, having to walk across ankle-deep water—this would all be part of swimming in the lowest flows since the very beginning of recording water in 1889.

WELCOME TO THE NEIGHBORHOOD

A river turns into a desert gradually: flow thins to trickle, then can disappear into the earth and sand altogether. But a desert can turn into a river in a flash. My hip-stubbing predicament seems to be the opposite of what Craig Childs, one of my favorite Southwest nature writers, encounters in the opening pages of his book, *House of Rain*. He's walking through a dry, barren canyon under a sizzling sun and endless blue skies when out of nowhere a flash flood roars through, turning parched earth into a waterslide. In a rare moment of ebullient recklessness, Childs jumps in: "The water felt like fists pummeling my body. As best I could, I floated with my boot tips sticking up, heading downstream, and my arms waving to keep myself straight... I tried to laugh aloud, but the cold water wrapped around my throat, and I could not let out anything but a gasp."

In his extensive writing and wanderings, Childs investigates what for centuries has been the biggest mystery in North American archaeology: Why the Ancestral Puebloans, the Anasazi, suddenly left their homes in the Four Corners region about 800 years ago. It just so happens I'm swimming through one of their old neighborhoods. In fact, the Anasazi were the last people to live in many of these canyons. One can still discover untouched vestiges of their civilization up in the nooks and crannies.

When we rounded the ominous-sounding Hardscrabble Bottom underneath Big Horn Mesa two hours before running into the sandbar, I knew that on top of the highest bluff stood an Anasazi lookout tower and granary built of neatly stacked slabs of sandstone filled in with clay mortar. All along this river, in places you'd never think to look—within secret side canyons, atop cliffside perches—you'll find signs of them. Caches in caves, granaries, arrowheads, campfire rings, kivas, implements, petroglyphs, pictographs, and pottery. As if they had just left to run an errand.

Their legacy is one of the biggest draws of this place, and it's much of what brings me back. It feeds my imagination as it did Edward Abbey's. The legendary (and, to some, infamous) nature writer and environmental activist was very clear about what sparked his curiosity. It wasn't the particular artifacts he may have found if he'd dug a little deeper on his rambles, but "the quality of that pre-Columbian life, the feel of it, the atmosphere." I think I know what he was talking about. If the afternoon sun stretches the present into timelessness, then this sun-baked desert pulls history into the here and now: every vista of these mesas and buttes evokes the Anasazi's beautiful, complex culture. One that thrived for centuries, then suddenly vanished like the wind.

I usually come to the Green River for a little R&R, and it seems I'm not alone in that; at one point in his book, Childs offhandedly refers to Canyonlands as the retirement home of the Anasazi. But after reading his account, no one would compare their intentions with mine. Childs explains that this harsh, desolate country was less of a vacation destination or Floridian snowbird oasis than it was a last resort for refugees. "The northernmost dead end for the Anasazi," in his words. Conflict over dwindling resources led to mass migration from far larger and more complex settlements at Chaco Canyon and Mesa Verde to the south. After living in cities of thousands bustling with culture and innovation, they came here in small groups, perhaps single families, to scratch out a living by hunting and gathering and damming seasonal streams in slot canyons to raise what few crops they could.

Follow the establishment of communal Ancestral Puebloan sites chronologically and you'll find that they become increasingly secluded and fortified. Despite its name, the Chaco Canyon settlement, considered the major cultural center at the height of Anasazi civilization, is wide open compared to the great houses etched into the cliffs at Mesa Verde. In turn, Mesa Verde, defensible as the relatively large settlement may have been, was a far cry more conspicuous and vulnerable than the ensconced outposts and guardhouses that protected the perfectly camouflaged dwellings here above the Green River.

Childs infers from their parapets a paranoia we moderns may associate with characters trapped in some kind of post-apocalyptic dystopia, as desperate to obtain precious resources as they are to evade threats that could come at any time from any direction. He writes, "Among the archaeological sites I have seen in Canyonlands, many are positioned in a way that makes me think the Anasazi were constantly checking their backs, keeping an eye on crucial points of movement in these canyons. Pressed by the thrust of war and overcrowding in the thirteenth century, they vanished into this hard, convoluted desert to escape the burning pith of their civilization. If you wanted to hide somewhere, guaranteeing no one would follow, this would be the place to go."

In *Desert Solitaire,* Abbey probes Anasazi psychology, surmising, "Fear: is that the key to their lives? What persistent and devilish enemies they must have had, or thought they had, when even here in the intricate heart of a desert labyrinth a hundred foot-miles from the nearest grassland, forest and mountains they felt constrained to make their homes, as swallows do, in niches high on the face of a cliff."

Today there is general agreement that the source of all the strife and suspicion was water, or rather, the lack of it. Through dendrochronology (tree-ring analysis), experts have determined that a major drought hit this region around the year 1200. The change in climate and precipitation likely pushed the Anasazi out of Chaco Canyon in search of more dependable water sources. Mesa Verde, and settlements like it, sprouted up, but the drought continued, civil war ensued, and eventually, those who stayed in the region fled here, the last outpost of a great civilization in decline. Others migrated south along the Mogollon Rim mountain range in Arizona and down the Sierra Madre Occidental range.

The sad story of their final departure from the Four Corners region has much to tell us today. Currently, I don't need to be scraping bottom on my strokes to know we are facing a mega-drought that is even more intense. It's been going on for two decades, and experts believe it's the worst in over a thousand years. Low precipitation levels are only partly to blame. Climate change has exacerbated the problem by desiccating the soil. This creates more dust, which melts the snow faster because it holds the heat instead of reflecting it. As we're getting less and less precipitation, more and more is needed to replenish drier and drier ground, and that limits the amount that flows back to waterways. This isn't a drought, which assumes it will end, but what scientist

Brad Udall, the senior water and climate scientist at Colorado State University, terms *aridification.* All of this accounts for the low flows Park Ranger Bego warned us about.

The Anasazi's relationship with water resonates all throughout Earth's living history. Back in the thirteenth century drought pushed them out. When Glen Canyon, which abuts Canyonlands, was dammed in 1963 to create Lake Powell, an inestimable number of their archaeological sites were drowned. It calls to mind the fossils excavated at Dinosaur National Monument 200 miles upriver on the Green River. About 150 million years ago, the thunder-lizard descendents of Tiklaalik perished due to a terrible drought before their bones were swept up by an equally colossal flood and deposited in a natural ossuary.

All of this drought and drowning prompts a stark realization that water demands a tricky balance: Too little, and you die. Too much, and you die.

CANYONLANDS

The barrenness of this place does not diminish its pull. In fact, I think it may strengthen it. People may not have lived here permanently since the Ancestral Puebloans, but they continue to be drawn back, and that includes my family and friends. After Powell's first expedition in 1869, he returned to float down the Green River again two years later, this time with a gaggle of artists and photographers to capture the occasion in enduring images, but mostly to finish measurements they had abandoned in favor of survival on the first trip.

It's easy to contrast our family's expeditions with Powell's. We have sunscreen, high tech gear, propane and stoves to conjure delicious dinners, and—thank god!—ice and cold drinks. Whereas Powell and his men roughed it, even by the rougher standards of their time.

But sometimes, a comparison between now and then is

warranted. One time, Kristin, Charlie, and I were enjoying the evening glow after dinner and the freedom of being still for a moment when all of sudden a microburst windstorm descended upon us and swept away our tent with Amelia inside. Ripped from the tent stakes, it tumbled down the beach toward the river. We bolted from our lawn chairs and sprinted to catch it. Once we stopped it, we unzipped the door and found Amelia sleeping soundly in a jumble of pillows and sheets, sleeping mats, and dry bags, as if nothing had happened. With heart pounding and adrenaline pumping, I was in the exact opposite state.

Over 150 years earlier, it was Powell's crew that weathered the microburst. "I go up to explore the alcove. While away a whirlwind comes, scattering the fire among the dead willows and cedar-spray, and soon there is a conflagration. The men rush for the boats, leaving all they cannot readily seize at the moment, and even then they have their clothing burned and hair singed, and Bradley has his ears scorched. The cook fills his arms with the mess kit, and, jumping into a boat, stumbles and falls, and away go our cooking utensils into the river. Our plates are gone; our spoons are gone; our knives and forks are gone." I know our little girl could've gone the way of Powell's utensils, and I'm eternally grateful we lucked out. You never know on the water. Just like life, situations can change in an instant.

At times, Powell's expedition sounds like a comedy of errors. After weeks of surviving on nothing but beans and rancid bacon, Powell and his crew came upon an island in the river and were delighted to find a garden with potato greens. They weren't so delighted after cooking and eating them for dinner, however. Potato greens can be toxic. The men became violently ill and had to take emetics. I'm grateful my closest river experience is a little indigestion after a lovely pre-made dinner—chili, lasagna, chicken piccata, etc. stored in a cooler and double-sealed freezer bags.

On those lazy family trips down the river, when we want a break from paddling at some point in the late afternoon, we often tie up the canoes and just let them drift. Someone breaks out an old waterlogged, duct-taped copy of Edward Abbey's *Desert Solitaire*, an entry point for those who become enamored of Canyonlands and the mythology of the West. Say what you will about Abbey, but the guy loved this part of the world and wrote about it in striking prose. The best place to read about the river is on the river, where currents of thought and water flow together. Whether or not you read aloud, the words seem to echo off the canyon walls. Our favorite chapter is "Down the River." Abbey writes,

> *We paddle our double craft into the current, ship paddles, lean back against the stern seats, which make good backrests and nothing much else, and smoke and talk. My anxieties have vanished and I feel instead a sense of cradle-like security, of achievement and joy, a pleasure almost equivalent to that first entrance from the outside--into the neck of the womb. We are indeed enjoying a very intimate relation with the river: only a layer of fabric between our bodies and the water. I let my arm dangle over the side and trail my hand in the flow. Something dreamlike and remembered, that sensation called deja vu-when was I here before? A moment of groping back through the maze, following the thread of a unique emotion, and then I discover the beginning. I am fulfilling at last a dream of childhood and one as powerful as the erotic dreams of adolescence-floating down the river. Mark Twain, Major Powell every man that has ever put forth on flowing water knows what I mean.*

In the early '50s, Abbey, accompanied by wife and kids, rolled into Moab all the way from New Jersey in an old pickup truck. He secured a job as summer ranger in Arches National Park, just north of Moab, and took up residence at Pack Creek Ranch in a miner's trailer depicted as basecamp in *Desert Solitaire*.

Working on an energy issue in Boulder, I was fortunate to meet the son of Bates Wilson, the first superintendent of Arches National Park who gave Edward Abbey the summer ranger job that would change his life and those of many of Abbey's readers. When Alan Wilson, a retired IBM engineer, heard about my love of Canyonlands and our yearly trips and swims, he shared his story.

Tug, as Alan is known throughout Canyonlands, moved to Moab with Bates and the rest of the family in 1949, when there was no Forest Service, not even a state highway. Tug remembers a classmate whose father flew him into town on a little plane so he could attend their K-12 school a few days a week. Back then, nearly everyone was in farming and ranching. There was a little hydropower and a single diesel generator that serviced Moab. Visitors had the option between two hotels and two cafes. Tourism wasn't even on the radar. When Bates Wilson suggested that folks might visit Arches and stay an extra night in a hotel, go out for dinner, and boost the local economy, denizens of Moab wondered why anyone would visit such a God-forsaken place to look at a rock with a hole in it.

Tug grew up in Arches in a single-room stone cabin with no electricity, no running water, and an outhouse. All roads leading to and from Moab were gravel and dirt. During the uranium mining boom, Tug wired little trailer units, including the one Abbey lived in, to house the miners. He also started Moab's first-ever guiding business taking customers out for $5 an hour in his cherished Jeep.

Tug told me that for all of Edward Abbey's contributions to environmental literature, he was always an irascible, controversial figure. He wrote about throwing beer cans out of his truck, and he wasn't kind to women, minorities, or anyone else for that matter. Tug's father gave Abbey his first job as a park ranger. Growing up during Abbey's time in Canyonlands, Tug has a different recollection of the writer than most. He spoke of Abbey living and writing along the borderland between fact and fiction, where reality ends and legend begins.

Abbey didn't publish *Desert Solitaire* until 1968—over a decade after he'd been in Canyonlands—and Tug thought that could account for some of the discrepancies. For instance, Tug doesn't remember the ramada, that shady, thatched-roof sanctuary from the sun, that Abbey writes so much about. Tug questioned if it even could have been built at all. You'd need to drill holes into the rocks to set the poles. Other stories such as killing a rabbit with a rock and roasting it for dinner (not only a serious violation of NPS policy but a stretch for anyone to imagine a hulking figure like Abbey catching a desert jackrabbit) or finding a dead body didn't quite match up with Tug's recollections, then or now.

Beyond appropriating other people's stories, Tug said, "Abbey had a big problem." He had a history of going off in the backcountry and driving in places he wasn't supposed to be and then getting stuck. "Ed Abbey was the worst park ranger they ever had," Tug told me. "He wrote well, but he was a total shit."

In the years directly after WWII, the arms race between the U.S. and the USSR ramped up and the market for uranium, a key element in building nukes, skyrocketed. The United States government subsidized mining expeditions all across the Southwest. Such incentives caught the attention of a budding young geologist Charlie Steen, who came up from Texas looking to get into mining. He asked Bates Wilson if he could look at his maps. By studying Wilson's maps, Steen figured out the best location to start digging. Turns out, Steen found one of the largest seams of uranium on the planet. The now-defunct mine sits right on the Colorado River at Potash Road, just a few miles from downtown Moab as a federally funded reclamation site.

For years, Bates took Tug and friends on Boy Scout pack trips to the "Land Between." They would travel on horseback through the area between the Green and Colorado Rivers. It was these early trips that inspired Bates to turn this majestic landscape into a National Park. In 1961, he invited Stuart Udall, Secretary of the Interior Department, to join him on the same horseback trip. Bates believed that if people set foot in this land and saw it for themselves they wouldn't just appreciate its beauty, they'd also want to protect it.

For many years in the '60s and '70s, Bates Wilson organized the 'Friendship Cruise.' The large flotilla of boats started at Mineral Bottom, went down the Green River and motored back up the Colorado River. In 1962, the Moab Chamber of Commerce held a public meeting to discuss the notion of turning Canyonlands into a National Park. Tug remembers that nearly every person was against it. The ranchers, the miners, even the Chamber itself. The only person really for it was Bates—and Stuart Udall.

Another key supporter was one of Utah's two senators, Frank Moss, who introduced a bill to create Canyonlands National Park. Immediately, controversy ensued, with the governor and other senator of Utah opposing. Miners and ranchers who had permits within the park were apoplectic. Many others joined the chorus of those who wanted to keep the area open for commercial use. In a significant turn of events, the Mormon Church added their support to the Moss bill and the idea of creating the park, but the battle dragged out for three years.

Some things never change, eh? This opposition to national parks and government protection of land would become a defining sentiment among certain factions in the American West. Some felt then—as they do now—that such policy is tantamount to a hostile government takeover of what belongs to the people. Land folks should be able to do what they darn well please with it. Even if that means tearing it up for minerals and then just up and leaving without any reclamation or clean up.

Despite protestations, President John F. Kennedy signed the proclamation creating Canyonlands National Park on September 14, 1964. Bates Wilson protected one of the most unique places in America and, in doing so, created a legacy that has enriched all our lives.

CHAPTER EIGHT

THE WATER DANCE

"As man has within him a pool of blood wherein the lungs as he breathes expand and contract, so the body of the earth has its ocean, which also rises and falls every six hours with the breathing of the world..."

– Leonardo da Vinci, Notebooks

Land and water have been in constant movement and change since the world was formed from a stew of matter.

As I look up to the tops of the canyon walls on the Green River, I see sculptures formed over the eons by weathering, erosion, and a whole lot of flooding. My mind drifts into the wet world of water, the reason I am able to swim here.

The water I'm swimming through on the Green River is here in southern Utah because storm systems developed over the Pacific Ocean and brought moisture eastward. First, these storms met the Sierras and Lake Tahoe. Then they traveled across deserts, where they held onto their moisture. Eventually, they met the formidable Rocky Mountains, and this is where they released moisture as precipitation—summer monsoons and winter snow.

When I swim, my thoughts invariably turn to the substance enveloping me, its unique structure and properties. Of course, I'm not alone in my curiosity. The water molecule continues to intrigue scientists, physicists, engineers, and hydrologists. H_2O is responsible for more commentary and speculation, more wonder and fear, than any other substance, any other molecule ever. Nothing even comes close.

On long swims, questions swirl in mental eddies:

Where does water come from?

What role does it play in Earth's origin?

What enables it to act as it does?

About 70% of the surface of the earth is covered in water, and of that, 96% is ocean and salt water. According to the United States Geological Survey, only 2.5% of all the water on earth is *freshwater*. Most of this water is locked up in ice and underground. Only 1.2% of this freshwater is available as surface water. Humanity is dependent upon a remarkably small, delicate amount of available water that isn't full of salt.

Since our bodies are 60% water, I suppose these questions naturally require further examination. Only after many, many hours of swimming, do I start thinking about this kind of heavy, existential stuff. Philip Ball, longtime editor of *Nature* and author of *Life's Matrix: A Biography of Water,* writes, "That we live on land is, in the grander scheme of things, best regarded as an anomaly, even an eccentricity—albeit with sound evolutionary justification. The story of life on Earth is, if we retain a true sense of proportion, a story of life at sea, and it is there that we must begin in order to really appreciate what water means to life."

WATER DEITIES

As the R & B legend of soul Roberta Flack sings, *"There is a river somewhere that flows through the lives of everyone."*

While they may have not been swimmers, the Ancestral Puebloans centered their lives around access to water, and they were not alone. All throughout human civilization, cultures, beliefs and religions have been based on water. Furthermore, water is used in many religious rituals—for baptism, ablution, consumption, and, in some cases, sacrifice. Water can symbolize purification, birth, and fertility—also drowning and death, thinking back to the Cave of Swimmers in Egypt. In most religious texts, water is considered holy.

Manthrams, a Hindu sect, worship water itself as a God and believe themselves to be "the Divine Water Souls." They believe bathing in the river washes away sins. Not merely water as a symbol, but a manifestation of a living God residing within them.

The largest religious ritual in the world is the Hindu *Kumbha Mela* festival, which occurs every 12 years. It is centrally, unequivocally focused upon water. It lasts several weeks and is spread over four sites. More than 200 million people attended in 2019, including 50 million on the festival's biggest day. Pilgrims come to take a ritual dip in the water because they believe it is a means of atonement for past transgressions. The water cleanses them of their sins.

Festival producers: take note of 50 million people celebrating water!

Water has given rise to deities the world over. To ancient civilizations, water could be a spirit, a god, a living being. In ancient Egypt, there is *Anuket*, the goddess of the Nile and nourisher of the fields. Her counterpart is *Sobek*, the god of the Nile, characterized as a man with the head of a crocodile. The Greeks had many deities. *Charybdis*, the spirit of the tides, was a sea monster. The most famous might be *Poseidon*, the Olympian god of the sea, floods, and drought. *Neptune* was his Roman equivalent.

Bali has a whole system of agriculture oriented around worshiping water with the statues of deities found at key water sources and irrigation points for fields.

In some South American cultures, the water goddess of fertility, home, and family, *Yemaya*, is both the constancy of life—its durability—and the change she engenders by creating life and altering it when necessary. Combining these contradictions, *Yemaya* is, more than anything, the protector of life.

In Hawaii, *Namaka* reigns as the goddess of the sea.

Kukulcan to the Mayans (*Quetzalcóatl* to the Aztecs) was a feathered serpent god who could whip up the seas, oceans, storms, and life itself.

There is something identifiable in being half-marine animal. What is a mermaid, after all, but a cocktail? A dash of *homo sapien*, a splash of fish... With our descendancy from the water, maybe the notion of a *Chimera*, half-serpent, half-lion, isn't so fantastical. Those who first conceived of the Chimera were drawing from somewhere deep within the double helix of DNA and a nearly forgotten vestige of our thunder-lizard origin. Maybe it was created to give meaning to the *aquaness* we still feel inside us; an innate sense of being *of* the water.

The development of these deities was a way of prescribing meaning to water, to give it a personality and recognizable features as a means of identifying with it. I find it fascinating that these gods were common in many great civilizations, societies, and tribes throughout time and around the world, but were mostly created independently of one another. Yemaya, Namaka, Kukulcan, Poseidon, and a Chimera are all spirits cut from the same cloth.

Maybe this is something Coco Robicheaux, the bayou hoodoo shaman, understood? As if the common blood of *Spiritland* was water. As a survivor of Hurricane Katrina, Coco knew all too well that water could also bring great harm. His bone-carved blessing was double-sided, which meant that one had to respect the power of water. Coco's talisman is fuel for my own torch.

Maybe these early observers and practitioners were on to something. Water, more than anything, seems to be worth worshiping. Worthy of immense respect and admiration. Something to organize a life and culture around. If water doesn't deserve its own sacrament, then what does? Could it be that water, in its liquid, vapor and crystallized forms, is the supreme gift to the universe? As it's the necessary element for the building blocks of

DNA—the very essence of life—I'd say so.

Water might just be the key ingredient of consciousness itself. No conception, no thought, no action can occur without water.

This is why water is our secret sauce, and it always has been.

Nineteenth-century German philosopher Ludwig Feuerbach noted, "Baptism has no validity and efficacy if it is not performed with water. Thus the natural quality of water has in itself value and significance, since the supernatural effect of baptism is associated in a supernatural manner with water only, and not with any other material. God, by means of his omnipotence, could have united the same effect to anything whatever. But he does not... Water is the purest, clearest of liquids; in virtue of this its natural character it is the image of the spotless nature of the Divine Spirit. In short, water has a significance in itself, as water. It is on account of its natural quality that it is consecrated and selected as the vehicle of the Holy Spirit."

Leonardo da Vinci's journals are filled with page after page of waves, riffles, and eddies. He was obsessed with the movement of water. He particularly loved the curl of a wave. In his close observations of human anatomy and the natural world around him, he often drew parallels, "The body of the earth, like the bodies of animals, is interwoven with ramifications of veins, which are all joined together and are formed for the nutrition and vivification of the earth and of its creatures. Its flesh is the soil, its bones are the arrangements of the connections of the rocks of which the mountains are composed. Its blood is the veins of waters; the lake of the blood, which is throughout the heart, is the ocean; its breathing and the increase and decrease of the blood through the pulses in the earth is thus: it is the flow and ebb of the sea."

With each stroke I take, the hydrogen bond of water yields a certain resistance and movement as it rearranges itself in the most beautiful of ways. It's the same swish that enraptured da Vinci. As my arms and legs propel through water, the tetrahedral shape of the molecules rejoin with other molecules. On every stroke, the molecules—or *little spirits*, as I think of them—reposition themselves with new partners again and again in a timeless dance.

CHAPTER NINE
THE CONFLUENCE

"The river flows
It flows to the sea
Wherever that river goes
That's where I want to be"
– Dylan/McGuinn

"I'm capable," I tell myself somewhere between Potato Bottom and Beaver Bottom with the Buttes of the Cross towering in front of me, "Capable of long swims, capable of beating the odds, capable of coming back from a broken leg..." At least, I believe I am, and maybe that's all that matters right now.

Sure, my pace has slowed down halfway to my destination here on the Green River, but all in all I'm in much better shape than I was when I powered through those 24.6 miles on Pontchartrain. Ok, sure, I'm older—there's that. Oh, and one other thing.

Several weeks earlier on a training swim in Moab with Mango and friends, I stepped out of the van in a funky way, and it wreaked havoc on my lower back. When I swam on the Colorado River from the Moab Boat Ramp to Gold Bar on the training swim for 15 miles, I could feel that pain climb up like venom from a snakebite.

The pull eventually concentrated in the intercostal muscle, which is sometimes called the invisible rib. It connects the latissimus dorsi to the ribs and beneath. When it gets jacked, the pain can be acute and lasting. Especially when you're sleeping, which is when the ribs compress. I've had it happen multiple times.

After the trip to Moab, I had to back off the training. For a minute, everything was in jeopardy just two weeks out. But a few days later, after resting, the pain abated.

Three hours into this swim, it starts up again, shooting from my lower ribs to my lat on the right side. Uh-ohhh.

By mile 14, it starts yelping.

Over 30 miles in, it's barking like a bad puppy dog.

"Come on, little shoulder," I whisper to myself. "You can do this."

Again, I've been through worse. And in that worse state, I applied the mindset I practiced with Mark Williams, which was ultimately healing. Instead of pushing difficult things away, I try to embrace them and make them part of the experience. By doing so, sometimes a negative becomes a positive. Embrace the shoulder.

We have another reason for hope. The Green River gathers steam as it nears meeting with the Colorado. In those last ten miles, the canyon narrows, the channel deepens, and the current picks up a little speed. I just have to get there to get a little push in the home stretch.

For now, I repeat what proved effective in those final brutal miles on Lake Pontchartrain: visualization, shifting my focus away from my pain and fatigue and to my destination until it leaps from my imagination into my field of vision. Eyes on the prize. A vision appears: at the beach where the Green River meets the Colorado River, I'm standing up, throwing my arms over my head, and embracing my family and team.

THE BRASS RING

Ah, the confluence... On every trip since the very beginning when Kristin brought the *Lagniappe* canoe into our life, the meeting of these two rivers has been a special place. It doesn't matter if we pull in at the end of a long five-day canoe trip, as soon as we arrive the hair stands up on the back of my neck and an energy sweeps through me.

After the high water surge of the spring runoff, a beach

will begin to form on either or both sides right where they meet. Generally, they are long, gentle, sandy beaches that arc along the river's curves, a hundred miles from nowhere. Access is nearly impossible from the Canyon Rim. The beaches at the confluence are some of the most beautiful in the entire world. Take it all in as you wheel around and you'll notice that as each river carved its respective canyons deeper and deeper, the dark red hue of the rock walls softens from deep vermillion, to French rosé, then ashen gray.

The contrast of these two flowing rivers meeting amidst such desiccation gives rise to the spirit and majesty of the place. The two snake together unannounced—they join around bends, so on each, you can't see the confluence until the last minute. Arriving at the meeting of the waters brings a sense of serendipity. As the olive-hinted Green River stirs with the ochre-tinged water of the Colorado River, it all seems like a beautiful cosmic coincidence.

Craig Childs shares my esteem for the place. In *House of Rain*, he steps over bighorn sheep manure on a narrow ledge when he notices what's below him:

> *From here the world looked as if it was falling apart around me, broken and heaved pieces of earth shaped into narrow fins. I had not found a vantage this high in nearly three weeks of poking around. I stopped under the open stage of the sky, the desert falling around me into impossible labyrinths. This was one of my home landscapes, Canyonlands, to which I returned often to walk the corrugated desert surrounding the confluence of the Green and Colorado rivers.*

This is not one of those rough-and-tumble collisions of two rivers playing chicken. Not a Big Bang but a soft whisper. An elegant courtship. A slow swirl with a loving touch. As if one river is looking over at the other and purring, "Well, hello there..." They do this dance for three miles, getting to know each other. Then just past a canyon called Dirty Devil Wash, they finally join for good and consummate at the first rapid, christened Brown Betty. Now the nomenclature is merely Rapid Number One. River maps produced after Cataract Canyon became a National Park only refer to the rapids as numbers.

Confluence of the Green and Colorado Rivers

Kristin likes to remind me that long ago the Colorado was called the Grand River from its source up in Grand Lake, Colorado, and the Green was called the Spanish River. Only after the confluence and the deep rouge hue of the water, would it be called the Colorado River, meaning "colored red" in Spanish. However, both names were changed for political reasons. (Isn't this the case in the naming of *all* places, not just rivers?) The naming of geography is highly political and subject to the culture of people who make up the names and write the maps.

Back in 1998, Kristin and I spent some memorable days together on the Colorado River. A few years had rolled by in graduate school and early careers. I had been living in Los Angeles working at Rock the Vote, a national voter registration campaign, mixing up music and politics. She was starting her career in water law practicing in Aspen. We weren't broken up, but we weren't living together either. Sort of a no man's land for a relationship. On our last night canoeing to the confluence, we looked at each other and knew what the other was thinking. The moment transpired as if we'd proposed to each other at once.

Let's get married!

At that point, we'd been together for six years, and maybe because of that the proposal was not the traditional, get-down-on-one-knee kind of thing as much as it was a flash of mutual understanding and agreement. Another confluence.

Floating down a river is fantastic. The only thing that beats it most of the time is swimming down a river. It's like they say in New Orleans—watching a parade is great fun; *being* in a parade is even better. Once over a dinner of chiles rellenos and margaritas in Santa Fe, Craig Childs confessed it hadn't even occurred to him that anyone would swim the rivers of Canyonlands—and likely it wouldn't have occurred to the Puebloans either. For them, the river would have been a place of deep foreboding, and there was no way to get back. As if they were spirits from the Cave of Swimmers, the river could be the source of life. Or a death wish.

I think of the river downstream of the confluence as the offspring of the Green and the Colorado upstream. I'm not going to say that the Colorado is the father and the Green is the mother or vice-versa. I'll just say that they're both necessary to create all that flows below where they merge.

Speaking of the Colorado, perhaps we should take a quick tour of the greatest river in the West...

The Colorado River starts at the top of La Poudre Park, right above the quaint little town of Grand Lake, Colorado, and just to the west of the Continental Divide, where a marshy meadow begins to divaricate into little streams. There are many other little rivulets that converge to form other streams that also flow into Grand Lake. There is also the controversial Grand Ditch that takes water up and over the Continental Divide in a transmountain diversion to send it to the Front Range, namely Denver and Aurora. This is the birthplace of the most important river in the West. East of the Mississippi, water is too plentiful. West of the Mississippi, it is too sparse. That's what makes the Colorado the most regulated and fought-over river in the world. Every drop of it has already been allocated before becoming a snowflake.

The river develops character and definition as it flows through Upper Gore Canyon and the eagle and osprey nesting grounds therein. Every summer a temporary little rafting community pops up at Rancho Del Rio on the section known as the 'Upper C.' This is where my son, Charlie, works his first rafting guide job the same summer as the Green River swim. Some days at the food truck a bluegrass band plays around the campfire and you can buy BBQ and cheap beer.

The river makes its way southwest and joins with the Eagle River, which some have argued is the true headwaters of the Colorado River. It rolls through sharp rock walls of Glenwood Canyon. It flows down the plateau and through Grand Junction (as in 'Grand River') where it meets with the Gunnison River. Then through Ruby Horsethief Canyon, where we have taken the *Lagniappe* canoe many times, the river enters Utah and into the raging rapids of Westwater. The river rolls past one of the original pioneer river crossings at Dewey Bridge, where it begins carving the magnificent canyons out of the soft sandstone of the Colorado Plateau. The river then snakes its way toward Moab, through Stillwater and Labyrinth Canyons. It continues towards the confluence, through Cataract Canyon and then into Lake Powell (what was Glen Canyon).

Afterwards, at Lee's Ferry, it dumps into the Grand Canyon. Later, it will hit Lake Mead, and much of it will be diverted to Las Vegas, San Diego, Los Angeles, and the Imperial Irrigation District. Siphoned off as it is these days, the Colorado River doesn't make it all the way to its true home in the Gulf of California anymore.

IF YOUR CAMP IS WIRED...

On the last night of an earlier trip, we pulled onto a small island in the middle of the Colorado river to make camp after a long day of paddling. Kristin and I were with our friends, Jennifer and Allen Blow from New Orleans, and we were all sunburnt and tired. At dusk, we set up our tents on a sliver of sand and began heating up dinner—homemade tempeh chili. Suddenly, wild winds swept through camp. We hoped the squall would pass, but the winds kept howling through the darkening canyon and getting stronger and stronger.

Uh ohh...

Intense weather was being pushed upstream from the Southwest, and the worst of it was headed directly for us. We halted dinner and covered it as best we could under the tarp with the other gear and then flattened the tents and secured them to the boats. We realized there was only one real option here: Sit on the point of our little island and simply be a part of the storm.

I'll grab the tequila!

We laid a tarp under our lawn chairs and folded it back over us as our only protection. With *Lagniappe* and the tent both lashed to my chair, the tempest of wind and rain roared through like a freight train. The canyons flashed with strikes of electricity of a hundred power plants. The hair stood up on the back of our necks as the infinite volts of white-hot current descended from the skies. Huddled beneath our flimsy tarp, we passed the bottle. Was this the end of us? Or the beginning of something else? Exposed on an island deep in the canyon a hundred miles from nowhere, we were feeling wet and wild. Our storm—we knew her well by now—swept over us, and we felt the immense energy. Her power seemed to emanate from the heavens.

This was no manufactured Disney experience. Sitting on that metal lawn chair in shorts, no shirt, and a sarong felt intensely real. We may have been anxious, but we weren't frightened. There wasn't much else to do.

Let's just take in the evening premiere of Earth's Best Weather Theater. Sit back, relax, and enjoy the show.

The lightning bolts resonated through our bodies. The clash of thunder. Howls of wind. Thrashing rain. All of it assaulted us. Kristin and I leaned in close, gripping each other's hand. Our fingertips jumped like a toad at every thunder strike.

Watching that storm was like watching history in the making. The canyons were alive with flash floods and a barrage of tumbling boulders. A Greek epic played out right before our very eyes. Poseidon, Zeus, and the rest of the Gods of earth, sky, fire, and water emerged from the corners of oblivion to assume their roles on the grandest of stages. For better or worse, we were front row.

We were not just watching this storm, we had become a part of it. The lesson we learned from that night would go on to become a defining tenet of our river trips and adventures henceforth: *If your camp is wired tight with everything tied down, loose items put away and camp buttoned up, the weather is a bonus.*

* * * * *

After the Lake Pontchartrain and Culebra-to-Puerto Rico swim, I set my sights on a first-ever swim down the Colorado River from Potash Point outside of Moab (launching point for most trips through Cataract) to the confluence for 47 miles. It was a much longer stretch of the river than any I had swum before, but because of our history with the river and our yearly trips, this was one swim that called to me. A whispering dream that wouldn't let go.

Like going through the epic storm, The Moab-confluence swim was the culmination of many river trips on the Colorado River. The first organized swim took place in 2001 with an experienced boater who had just rowed down the Grand Canyon.

As I was about to start our 15-mile swim from the Moab boat ramp to a nice little camp spot at Gold Bar, the boatman, Earl Rogers, owner of New York Pizza in Aspen, insisted I wear a life vest.

"Keep up!" I laughed, then jumped in and started swimming.

The Colorado River swims kept building. In the summer of 2006, I assembled a group that included Mango and a few others. I planned a swim that I guessed would take place over two days. This was way back when I had a much narrower understanding of everything endurance swims entailed. You could say my comprehension of the very word, "endurance," was in the infancy of its long, hard-earned development. I thought I just needed to go out and swim a lot. I didn't have a coach, and I didn't even know how long I would be in the water. By contrast, that first big swim trip would offer a few pointers about how to put this kind of larger adventure together the right way. But I can't say it wasn't eventful.

We did manage to make it in two full days of swimming. No one who experienced those two days would call them "pretty." There were arguments. A lot of partying among the crew. A plague of bugs. The raft had trouble keeping up with me swimming. One friend decided he wanted to swim instead of paddle. The problem was he fell way behind along with another johnny-come-lately who didn't even have goggles. We had to wait a while for them, and I was cold and upset that they would put the whole swim in jeopardy. *"What's the point?"* I thought to myself. *"How am I ever going to make it to the confluence*?" I told them all this, but not in such friendly terms. It might be more accurate to say I lost my shit.

Instead of continuing to argue I snapped my goggles into place and dove back in and resumed swimming. *Screw 'em.*

We finally got it together as a team on the second day. I learned a valuable lesson from that experience, one I would learn the hard way (code for "again and again"): sometimes your friends or family members don't make the best support crew.

When, at last, we reached the confluence, I wolfed down

soup straight from the can. Mango got busy making dinner and everyone else started making camp as the sun set against the crooked walls of the confluence. After several hours of recovery and repast, we gathered around the campfire for cocktails. The hard feelings floated away like the embers. And, oh, what embers on this particular night! Tracing fantastic curlicues in the dark. Fiery calligraphy. Were they always so mesmerizing? Why hadn't I noticed before? And what was in the Nalgene bottle with the electrolytes? Something very strange.

A tickle crawled up from the bottom of my spine, gained momentum as it neared my solar plexus, and blossomed into a massive leonine yawn. Stars began popping out like silvery blueberries against the azure of the universe. Deep in the canyons alone we let ourselves be wild. We ran across the beach. Spun big sticks with the ends lit on fire. We laid upon the sand and submitted to the forces of gravity. Marveled at the dynamic, spinning night sky. Howled at the moon. A state of exhaustion coupled with euphoria. We were psychonauts with synapses firing on all cylinders.

We all agreed that out in the wild, nothing else matters. The paint job on the house. The work memo. The tires on your car that need rotating. Most of it just washes away with the river current, everything rendered irrelevant by the magnanimity of the universe unfolding before us.

But it's more than that. We must accept we're doomed and find a way to live with it. Once we accept the doom, chaos, and destruction, there can be liberation. It's not a new notion, of course, but it rang with a certain clarity under the stars. Don't hold on to things so tightly. Floods, drought, famine, volcanoes, and tornadoes have all happened before and will happen again. People change, for better and worse. They will impress you. And they will disappoint you. Life happens, so let it. Resilience, durability—call it what you will. Whether it is a global pandemic, conflict, resource shortage, or whatever else, *the time has come to toughen up.*

We must stop stressing out so much by accepting the things we cannot change and doing what we can with what we have. Don't give up. Charge forward.

* * * * *

That night on the river was a gift. Transformation happens out there in the canyons. On the water. On any adventure really. Take experience, hardship, elation, top it off with a dollop of love and friendship and, behold! *Meaning*. After all those nights on the rivers and swimming around the world, I have realized the shared experience of those early swims forged lifelong bonds. A swim isn't even a metaphor for life. It's the real thing. When an adventure begins, it ripples through water, but it also ripples through people.

* * * * *

On my swim down the Colorado River six years prior to the Green, Kristin had paddled her own kayak the entire way with Mark Williams, Allen Blow, who had endured the storm with us on the little island while we huddled in our lawn chairs, and legendary ski photographer Tom Winter. Kristin had played the same role as Mike Fiebig scouting up ahead to find the fastest current. In August 2015, after many years in the making, it was as if all my history in Canyonlands of the past 20 years had come full circle. After 47.5 miles (76.4 km) in 13 hours 56 minutes of swimming, I stood up on the beach at the confluence and raised my arms over my head in near darkness.

Over the years, the confluence has served as the setting to some of the most important events in my life. You get a sense of why this area was sacred to tribal nations who inhabited it for millennia. It's a place that has changed me. Sure, it's the locale itself, but it's also the journey of getting there. The confluence is not easy to access, but once you arrive, the majesty and historical significance of two rivers meeting in the stark, barren desert unfurl before you.

CHAPTER TEN
WATER HEAD

"Somebody may beat me, but they are going to have to bleed to do it."

– Steve Prefontaine

The notion of swimming the Green River had been swirling in my head for a few years, and with nine months to go, I was still a little reluctant to jump in with both feet. Around Thanksgiving of 2020, I was waffling. Frankly, I was feeling overwhelmed and intimidated. The previous year of life had been a whirlwind. I had just turned in the manuscript for my book, *Ignition*. A change of job had thrown me for a loop. Kids. Life. Need any more excuses? Kristin, always the sensible one, encouraged me to start training seriously.

"You're better when you're busy," she noted.

Of course, she was right. She knows me better than anyone. I'd be a raving madman if I didn't swim. The Green River swim was also a way to set a goal, train, get fit, and keep my sanity in a global pandemic.

In November, 2020, I began swimming with Josiah Middaugh, who has won the 2015 Xterra World Championships and is a 15-time national Xterra champion. He is simply a bad-ass athlete. The man has "Everested" a bicycle climb, meaning that on one ride he climbed 29,032 feet, the distance from sea level to the peak of the world's tallest mountain. Considering that he was inducted into the Xterra Hall of Fame as the one of the greatest off-road triathletes in the history of the sport, Josiah is remarkably humble. I was honored that he appreciated what I was putting together.

We had already postponed the swim for a year due to

the COVID-19 pandemic. Then I started thinking, *What if this is actually the perfect time to train*? Probably the safest place to be was in the water. Josiah and I met for coffee and set out some initial goals. He developed the loose arc of a training plan. He would assign workouts weekly. He wanted to keep it somewhat flexible, but keep to a general time frame with milestone swims leading up to the main event. There would be a series of long, crushing Saturday endurance swims in January and February with a training camp in April and a few open water swims along the way. After the initial excitement of committing to the swim and working with Josiah wore off, the realization of just how much I needed to train over the next six months set in.

Our Saturday workouts consisted of a 6K, then an 8K, a 7K, a 9K, and back to a 6K. Then a threshold 12K to pack on the distance. I would swim five to six times a week, coupled with two days a week of dryland exercises in the gym to build muscle and core strength. I also skied at least one or two days a week. I admit, I should have been doing more yoga and stretching; perhaps that omission had something to do with the screaming intercostal muscle.

Training Camp in late April was the most intense of all. Reserving pooltime in a pandemic was memorable.

"I need four hours on Wednesday," I said.

"Umm, OK..." Since they only book in one-hour increments, the athletic club operator found it an odd request.

"OK, cool... and can I get another four hours for the following three days?"

"Uh... I'll have to check with the manager," she replied.

SWIM FROM THE BELLY

The benefits of open water swimming are numerous, and they extend beyond the confines of a pool. One specific benefit offers another handy response to the *Why?* question. I wouldn't say I'm doing physics problems in my head when I'm swimming, but concentrating on staying balanced and streamlined, kicking up and down in unison with arms rotating 'round and 'round is a cognitive exercise. *Thinking.* Swimming may come naturally after years of repetition, but the mind must still process all the elements involved in the total action. At times, I'm thinking about work or personal issues, but many times I'm just thinking about putting one arm in front of the other. Breathing. Racing at different paces at different intervals requires even more thought.

With all these various cognitive functions working in tandem, swimming helps to optimize brain function and health. Coaches can see it in champion swimmers and in youngsters who are just learning. The focus it brings and the regulated breathing explain my parents' decision to put me in the pool so long ago. I know what it does for me, and my wife says she sees it in me too, God bless her.

Science backs her up. Numerous studies show swimming has many health benefits, from slowing down aging, to improving mental health and brain function, to easing the simple act of getting out of bed to improve yourself. And then there's *interleaving*, a way to rearrange memory to increase performance. It's a concept borrowed from the fields of computer science and telecommunications, but it can also be applied to swimming. Steven Munatones explains, "In open water swimming, interleaving is an approach that stresses the use of the body and mind in a non-contiguous way to increase mastery of skills, help in motor learning, and improve memory recall."

For open water swimmers, interleaving may comprise drills that train different aspects of the stroke such as pulling, kicking, sculling, sprints, and distance—maybe even all in the same workout. Munatones points out that interleaving includes the use of the four major strokes—butterfly, backstroke, breaststroke, and freestyle—and incorporates "working on pacing, navigating, positioning, feeding, sighting, dolphining, and drafting in a workout, performed in a pool and an open body of water." He advocates training in various settings, such as in the morning during tranquil conditions, but also when the wind howls and the chop pounds you in the face. He goes on, "Interleaving stimulates stress that then leads to the secretion of corticotropin-releasing factor (CRF) in the brain's hippocampus where memory and learning are centralized and improved." Given such brain function benefits, I'm glad I also enjoy hiking, road cycling, and cross-country skiing. I enjoy slow burn sports and, after my experience shattering my leg, keeping my feet on the ground.

"Swimming is multimodal," Munatones says. He believes swimming brings together all of those exercises. When we do a swimming practice with a warm up, stroke work, kicking, and standard interval training with all four strokes, it neatly combines aerobic intensity, resistance, and skill-based training. Similarly, swimming in the sea, ocean, and lake provides for this variety of training.

In all swimming, but especially long distance swimming, posture and positioning are critically important for efficiency. My old swimming friend Spencer Hawkins, who swam for UC Berkeley, told me once, "You've got to swim from the belly." He meant that you shouldn't swim solely from the shoulders with your butt dragging underwater and your legs trailing. With head and neck extended upward, swimmers look like they're swimming uphill. As if they're fighting. Practically speaking, they are.

This type of "uphill" swimming is a good way to overstress the shoulders. Instead, think of swimming downhill. Start with the head well-positioned and relaxed, like when you're standing up straight. Then imagine the crest of your butt skimming the top of the water. To get the butt up, the legs have to be moving as an integral part of the stroke. They can't be dead weight dragging behind you. A good swim stroke is a whole body experience from fingertips to toes. Efficiency is the name of the game with each rotation attaining the maximum distance per stroke (DPS). How far can one arm reach as it is propelled by the other arm until it then takes over and begins the next rotation? Many coaches describe the perfect pull as reaching over a barrel of whiskey. Not an "S-curve" of the old style that sweeps across the chest as it finishes, but an "I-stroke," a clean line rolling over into a straight high-elbow pull through to the finish past the buttocks. The beauty of swimming is that, if done right, the whole self becomes a symphony of movement. Instead of sound, it produces propulsion. When racing and on long distance endeavors, every cell in your body turns toward that purpose. No thought other than *forward*. There is an immediacy about racing and big swims. About most athletic endeavors, for that matter. Events like swimming the Green River or swimming in competition bring a sense of urgency and a deadline. When submerging into the water, all the body is thinking about is NOW. Nothing else matters.

* * * * *

One day after practice, Josiah and I talked about how people—and especially athletes—can create a lot of drama. They get stuck inside their head. They go down rabbit holes of distraction, and that takes energy away from what matters: the training. Hey, I'm just as guilty as the next person. Especially before a race. One time when I was getting all worked up about the swim and tasting a little fear in the back of my throat, Josiah said something like, "It's going to be like every other day of your life. You are going to put on your suit and goggles. Put your toes in the water and go. You'll swim until you're finished, and then you'll get out. That's basically it."

Like every other day of my life, but maybe a little longer.

FEEDING STICK

On every swim, when Mark blows the whistle twice, it's time for another feeding, a term that cracks up Kristin, who thinks it sounds like it's time to throw food to animals at the zoo. My feedings usually occur every 20 to 25 minutes. For the Green

River swim, we planned on having between 30 and 35 feedings. Nutrition, along with physical training and mental conditioning, is one of the three legs of the stool. And probably my weakest.

Sometimes I wonder if I work so hard in the water to give myself an excuse to carry on splurging outside the water. Before a big swim or a race, my go-to dish is shrimp in a white wine butter sauce with asparagus, fresh tomatoes, and basil. But in civilian life, I love fried catfish, lasagna, enchiladas, pizza, chicken piccata, blackened redfish stuffed with crabmeat and topped with a meunière sauce. Once my New Year's Eve resolution was to have *more* sauce with my meals—and that's one resolution that's stuck. *Extra side of béarnaise, si vous plait*. I can make a gumbo ya-ya that would make my momma proud. Red beans and rice. Boiled crawfish. On many a night, I enjoy a glass or more of wine. Tito's vodka with soda and a splash of cranberry juice and lime is my go-to cocktail.

Turns out, Josiah wasn't too concerned about my diet. I was already losing weight through the training, and he didn't want me losing too much and then being more susceptible to the cold water. *Ah yes, this was one of the few times in life when a little extra cushion had advantages.*

Mark prepared the old beat-up soft body cooler we've used on swims for over a decade. In went Bobo's Oat Bars, scrambled eggs, gels, Honey Stinger waffles, a few bean and cheese burritos, and other sundry treats, including those leftover chicken lettuce wraps. In addition, he packed a few gallons of water, electrolytes, and a protein drink mix. When I find something that works, I stick with it. Most long distance swimmers use only liquid protein/electrolyte fuel drinks. I find ultra-distance athletes have been turning away from purely synthetic foods. Gels are fine for a race of a few hours, but for anything longer, a body needs real food.

My strategy is to eat only a little—about 100 calories at each feeding—but frequently keep the tank topped off and wash it all down with lots of electrolytes and water. Even if the body doesn't feel dehydrated or thirsty, drinking water is key to your survival on a long swim. Without it, the other foods won't properly digest. Dehydration in water is an awful irony.

Other swimmers are different. People generally find what works for them, and they adapt to it. Sarah Thomas drinks a blend of mostly carbs with a dash of protein and electrolytes every 30 minutes and supplements with solid food as needed.

Eating while swimming is not natural. Our bodies are not adapted to eat while we're in the water. When we're swimming, we don't feel hungry. We may be ravenous when we get out of the water, but not in it. And that poses a real challenge because, of course, the human body is like a car: it doesn't matter how finely tuned the engine is, if it lacks fuel, it won't go.

Once "the bonk" happens, there's no coming back. The only way to train for this very thing is by eating in the water. On long pool swims, instead of hanging on the wall, I'd tread water at the deep end and eat between sets. Paradoxically, the longer the swim, the more frequent the feedings.

After two short blasts of the whistle, Mark will move slightly ahead and prepare the feeding stick, which consists of two bottles with carabiners attached to ropes. In its small, shallow net he'll arrange several options, including whatever I suggested during the previous feeding. I swim up to the stick, reach over, take a few bites of a bar, stuff some scrambled eggs in my face, and wash it down with water and electrolytes. This is our chance to communicate, but usually it's dine and dash. After gulping, I'll leave the water bottle floating and start swimming again. (We've learned our lesson—once, during a water bottle handoff, the canoe tipped.) Mark usually hangs back and takes a moment to reorganize everything. He repacks the feeding stick into the kayak and zips up the cooler. He also notes the next feeding time and writes down the log. As soon as he's done, he catches up as quickly as possible. Feeding needs to be efficient and takes coordination and organization.

Feeding time

When the yardage is long and hard, the question that resounds loudest sounds like that of a curious child is *Why?* But a few other questions continually pop up for endurance athletes: *How far can you really push yourself? Or do you need to? What do we need to prove and to whom—if at all? When is it over the edge?* Undoubtedly, there are times when people push it too far. Hungarian swimmer Attila Mányoki writes in his book, *Oceans Seven: How I Cheated Death and Broke the Hardest Record in Swimming,* about his attempt to cross the stretch of water between Ireland and Scotland called the North Channel—widely considered the most difficult of the Oceans Seven Swim, seven of the world's most famous open water swimming challenges. The others are not exactly easy, swimming from England to France across the English Channel, the wild currents of the Tsugaru Strait in Japan, the wildlife of the Catalina Channel, the sharks of the Cook Strait between the North Island and South Island of New Zealand, the Molokai (or Ka'iwi) Channel between Molokai Island and Oahu Island in Hawaii with all sorts of dangers, and the Strait of Gibraltar. With the Scottish shore in sight on the North Channel, Mányoki blacked out. He woke up days later in a hospital and barely lived through the experience. Amazingly, he returned the following year and completed the swim.

Ram Barkai, who swims in the coldest water on earth, founded the International Ice Swimming Association. In 2008, he swam 1 kilometer in southernmost Antarctica in water that was between 0 and 1 degree Celsius, earning him recognition from the Guinness Book of World Records.

I met him at the World Open Water Swimming Conference on Rothesay Island off Scotland in 2014. We talked over dinner one night about the very real dangers of zero-degree swimming. Swimming for 20 minutes in freezing water is one challenge, but the real danger may be getting out, when a potentially dangerous condition called afterdrop develops. This occurs when your body begins to warm up and it can be extremely painful as you shiver uncontrollably. This is when cardiac arrest can come knocking at your door. However, Barkai also explained that over years and years of practice and adaptation, the body adjusts and becomes more tolerant. The human body is an amazing machine in how fast it can adapt to changing conditions, both cold and hot—something we may need to think about more in the future.

Sarah Thomas, 40, has completed a string of jaw-dropping firsts in marathon swimming. A key one was swimming 80 miles from Bullfrog to Wahweap in Lake Powell in 2016. In 2017, she set the record for the longest continuous, unassisted, current-neutral swim at a whopping 104.6 miles in Lake Champlain. That swim took more than 67 hours. Shortly after, she was diagnosed with an aggressive form of breast cancer. But she tackled that challenge as she would a major swim, and less than a year after completing treatment, she became the first person in history to swim four times across the English Channel continuously for 82.5 miles in 54 hours and 10 minutes. *Four times in a row!*

I caught up with her at her day job in human resources and

just before she was leaving for a successful *double* crossing of the North Channel. (Mányoki nearly died doing it once.) She told me it wasn't so much about what other people have done, it's about finding out what you can do. How far can you push yourself? The answer to this burning question for all endurance athletes also answers the *Why*?

Sarah Thomas often gets asked if she prefers the process or the end result, a swim's finish? "Definitely the process," she says. "Glory is fleeting. It's the *process* you live with, day in and day out."

* * * * *

Discovering maximum limits of endurance seems to be part of some people's DNA. For them, the question is not *Why?* but *Why not?* Nature offers such folks plenty of inspiration. For example, there's the godwit, a lovely little bird deserving of celebration. In search of an endless summer, it makes the longest migration of any animal on Earth. Each year, the bar-tailed godwit flies 7,000 miles from Alaska to New Zealand, where it raises offspring, and then flies back again. It soars non-stop for 8 to 10 days without food or water. It flaps night and day sometimes through high winds and pounding rain. The flight has confounded researchers and challenged all assumptions about endurance. Simply put, it should not be happening.

Robert E. Gill, a biologist with the U.S. Geological Survey in Anchorage, who has studied the godwit for almost 50 years, remarks, "I tell people, 'Try exercising for nine straight days—not stopping, not eating, not drinking,' to convey what's going on here. It stretches the imagination."

The godwit is not only the world's mightiest endurance athlete, it is also equipped with superior navigation abilities. Some researchers believe these birds can sense magnetic lines across the planet in a process called quantum entanglement. And they are expert weather forecasters. Dr. Gill says they know what conditions are best for departing and which winds are most favorable. "They can piece the puzzle together in terms of what the conditions are in Alaska and between there and Hawaii, between Hawaii and Fiji, and between Fiji and New Zealand."

What inspires me most about these birds is their adaptability. Before their flight, their body and organs undergo a restructuring. The kidneys, livers, and gizzards shrink and become lighter. Their pectoral muscles expand to support constant flapping. Then they eat and eat and eat to double their weight. Dr. Gill compares them to obese super-athletes.

As these birds and countless other examples throughout nature can attest, we who share this planet possess a remarkable capacity to adapt and summon extraordinary feats of endurance. We can figure out how to survive in even the most difficult of circumstances, whether it be in water, on land, or in the air.

* * * * *

As with most everything, in discovering our physical endurance, there's a balance we have to strike. For many swimmers, both in the pool and in open water, the act itself can be singularly focused. Which is a good thing up to a point—at least, for me. Too tight of a focus becomes tunnel vision, myopia. Taking it all *too* seriously can suck all the joy out of an adventure. A swim without humor or humanity just isn't my style. I have seen so many swims that appear to be the opposite of fun. Just sufferfests.

At the same conference in Rothsay, Scotland, where I met Barkai, I sat through a presentation by a group of Russian swimmers who completed a relay across the Bering Strait. People nearly died. They ran out of toilet paper on an old ship with little heat and survived on borscht. Congratulations to them, but it looked absolutely miserable. No one was smiling.

My torch is a little different. I want my swims to be joyous occasions. "Dancing in the water," as David Amram described it when he sang. Even in their toughest moments, my swims are a celebration and a way to bring attention to water.

LIGHT AS A FEATHER

A person can train their body to swim for 15 hours straight. But the longer the swim, the more of a mental game it becomes. The greater the duration, the greater the pain, which gives more opportunity for self-defeating thoughts to creep in. Training in the pool and in the gym would only take me so far. Swims of this magnitude demand more than just physical training; they also require mental conditioning. Endurance swimming comes down to mind over matter.

On these endurance swims, you cross into unknown territories. Each stroke, each mile, feels like pushing the Sisyphean rock up the hill one more time. In these moments, will you curse the gods or will you recognize your own agency and keep going? When you're shitting yourself and seizing up with cramps, will you find the tenacity to smile? Moments like these, which offer us the freedom to fail, make us who we are. They arise from a wide range of challenging endeavors—sailing across the ocean, free-diving to the deepest depths, or riding the biggest wave. These moments of freedom and failure also occur in the boardroom, while running a restaurant, closing a big deal, and a million other ways. Mine happen to come through swimming.

What do I mean by *mental conditioning*? As Mark Williams explains, it's not sitting cross-legged on cushions and blissing out. He gives me "sets for the mind" the same way Josiah might assign me sets in the gym. These mental exercises can be grueling as well. We practice narrowing the mind's focus to a point like a laser beam or widening it to take a 360° view of any given situation like a hunter stalking prey.

For many years during the lead up to the Green River swim I adopted the mantra, *light as a feather.* A deep inhale on *light* and a long slow exhale on *as a feather.* This was my go-to phrase to recenter myself and push away distractions. I used it in visualizations and in training. I could see myself as a little white feather effortlessly bobbing along on top of the river. I picked the phrase because it could be a life motto. Don't get bogged down. Don't get overwhelmed. Be nimble. Adjust to rapidly changing circumstances. Roll with the punches. *Light as a feather.*

I repeated it enough to myself in training that I've mentally applied it to just about every aspect of life. Dealing with difficult people, managing stressful situations, and making better decisions. Sometimes to calm down, I'll take three deep belly breaths, close my eyes, and repeat, *light as a feather*, to center myself.

These mental conditioning techniques can be applied to enhance awareness and performance. Mark and I practice more complex exercises, but *light as a feather* is a simple way of expressing it. Much of mental conditioning is about disciplining your thoughts and visualizing your performance. Over time, through the physical workouts and preparation, you chisel yourself into someone ready to meet the challenge.

In my book on communication strategy, *Ignition,* I write about the 'Locus of Control,' whereby we create the mental conditions to believe we can accomplish an endeavor. Are we in control of our destiny—or are we merely the subject of external forces? Can we control the factors in our environment or do we merely react to situations we had no say in creating? Planning and organizing these swims is a way for me to exercise control over my own life and plan my own adventure, even while realizing that many things are beyond my control—from swimming to the wrong island to finding alligators sunning themselves at the finish line.

This isn't a tour operation or an all-inclusive vacation. I'm not handing over the reins so that I can sit back and rest easy, free from the responsibility of decision-making. There's no 'cruise ship mentality' here, no experience scrubbed clean of stress and discomfort. Rather, adventure swimmers choose to take control of their own destiny, with all the storms, gyres, currents, sunrises, and sunsets that such a destiny entails.

This unpredictability is what distinguishes adventure swimming from other sports and why it requires great mental acuity. I believe *adventure swimming* entails arranging your own support and logistics on a river, lake, or ocean. This might be on water that no one has ventured to swim, or, at least, very few people. It means assembling your own team and determining a unique start and finish. Adventure swimming usually still follows Captain Matthew Webb's approach. One can follow the recognized rules and regulations of the Marathon Swimmers Federation and WOWSA and set records and claim firsts across bodies of water that seem impossible. But, hey, the real point of adventure swimming is that it's your own experience. Wade along the shore, wear floaties, do water ballet, swim naked, or whatever else floats your boat. In adventure swimming, the beauty is that you can swim however you like.

* * * * *

I asked Sarah Thomas, likely the greatest distance swimmer the world has ever known, about the mind game. She told me that she had spent a lot of time thinking about this question. She said she had never done any formal mental conditioning coaching, but she thinks it is about 70% to 80% of the whole effort. For her, the important thing in training is getting your mind to a place where quitting is simply not an option.

"Maybe I'm miserable and not having a ton of fun. I know if I'm in danger or conditions aren't good, they'll pull me out," she said. "But when it comes to me, or a personal choice, quitting is something I'm not allowed to do."

Distance swimmer Lori King, who was the first to swim the 24 miles from Block Island to Montauk in 8 hours and 39 minutes in 2022, fighting severe cramps, sweeping currents, and curious sharks along the way, told the *New York Times,* "I had to tell myself, 'You just have to be comfortable with being very uncomfortable.'"

Thomas believes that few people have taught themselves to deal with pain and push through discomfort. "Humans are conditioned to want to be comfortable. We want to be well fed and we want to be dry. So, when all of a sudden we find ourselves in these situations when we're not warm and we're not dry and we're not well fed and we're tired, the natural inclination is to want to stop and get out." Sarah's technique involves doing frequent body scans of herself. She said if her limbs are functioning—arms are moving, elbows and hands feeling fine—then everything is okay. Just being cold and uncomfortable isn't enough to quit.

When a swim gets especially arduous, she says to herself, "I'm tough. I'm strong. I can take it."

As we talk, Sarah says something I can relate to all too well, "It's your mind that tells you it needs to quit. Not the body."

She says she came close to stopping on Lake Powell during her second full night of swimming, but her team encouraged her to just make it to the next feeding. And the next feeding. And the next. She kept going. And going. She became the first person to swim 80 miles across Lake Powell. It took her 56 hours and for some of those hours she wanted out. But she didn't quit.

* * * * *

Sometimes during training it felt like I was rehearsing for a big theatrical performance. Other times I imagined I was working my way toward a big international competition. No matter how I conceived of them to extract the most inspiration, those early months of 2022, six months out from the Green River swim, were key to preparing my body and spirit for endurance.

After signing up and putting in all the work and training, making all the investment, you eventually discover *IT'S*

HAPPENING. Game on. People have gathered to support you. Have fun. Be grateful you're there. It will be tough and grueling, but those who can smile in the face of such pain and suffering are those who prevail. As Josiah says, "The race *is* the reward."

I put four years of planning into this Green River swim, and I'd only be in the water for less than a day. In that context, the swim wasn't all that long, really, an almost infinitesimal fraction of my life. I wanted to savor every minute, every stroke. I wanted to make the moment last as long as possible.

The techniques of conditioning your mind apply just as much to everyday life as to endurance sports. They are the same techniques Mark Williams used when flying F-15s in combat over Baghdad. They're the same fundamentals used by Josiah Middaugh in winning world championships. The same mindset used by Sarah Thomas to swim the longest distances in the history of mankind. And who knows, maybe it's what the bar-tailed godwit uses to fly all those thousands of miles.

The principles are similar: Setting a big audacious goal and training for it. Doing the hard work. Preparing and training. Performing. Building a team and support crew. Believing in yourself. Adopting an internal Locus of Control. And, ultimately wading into the water and swimming from one end to the other.

These lessons I take from swimming adventures and give to life, family, friends, and career. The water has much to teach all of us.

CHAPTER ELEVEN

PURA VIDA SWIMMING ON THE GULFO DULCE

The sun had just begun peeking over the horizon at 5:00 a.m. in Costa Rica's steamy Golfo Dulce as my goggles snapped into place and I waded into the warm water. Call me easily amused, but I love the sun rising or setting on these swims as markers of time. Separating day from night, dark from light. These moments of transition often reflect what's going on in our own lives. Especially mine at the moment because a 21-kilometer swim lay ahead. For this swim, I wasn't alone; 10 racers from around Latin America and the U.S., most of us painted white with zinc and layered with grease to ease the chafing, waded in to start, each with our own support kayaker.

But sloths, not swimming, was what brought my daughter, Amelia, and me to the sultry jungles of the Osa Peninsula. Amelia was turning 11 on August 3rd, the day of the race. For Christmas, Santa Claus gave us a Father-Daughter trip for sloth sleuthing. Naturally, I thought about opportunities for a little adventure swimming.

The Golfo Dulce (Sweet Gulf) is a large bay tucked between the Osa Peninsula and the mainland in remote southern Costa Rica. Go any further south and you run into Panama. Because it's shielded from the open ocean of the Pacific, the gentle waters of the Golfo Dulce are home to whales who calve there, dolphins seeking refuge, turtles laying eggs, and many other species who thrive and propagate among the coral reefs.

Long ago, the finger of the Golfo Dulce peninsula was an island off the coast of Costa Rica. Over millions of years, the water level gradually fell, revealing a land bridge attaching it to the mainland at the southern end of Costa Rica. It is home to Corcovado National Park, which has some of the greatest biodiversity on the planet. Matapalo, where the ocean meets the Gulfo Dulce, is a well-known surfing spot.

I first heard about the swim from Joanie Kleypas, a marine ecologist with the National Center for Atmospheric Research in Boulder, Colorado. Joanie experiments with growing and harvesting coral in the Golfo Dulce to replenish and strengthen endangered reefs. We swim together with the Boulder Aquatic Masters swim club. She mentioned the Golfo Dulce race, correctly assuming it would appeal to me. I love swimming in beautiful and unique places, and this sounded like Eden. A wild jungle both above and beneath the water.

Jafet Montero was assigned as my *kayakista*. We hit it off from our first conversation. For generations his family has owned the bakery in the small town of Puerto Jimenez. He rises at 2:00 each morning to bake bread before heading off to his day job as a nature guide in Corcovado National Park and the expansive jungle just outside our door.

For two days prior to the race, Jafet and his girlfriend (now wife), Adri, took us around to see sloths, monkeys, and other wildlife. We bounced along for miles in a little two-door 4×4 Suzuki we called "*Blanco Jimmy*" on back roads and across streams you couldn't find in any guidebook. Jafet could spot the tiniest black speck of something nestled in a tree. He would set up a little tripod telescope with an upward facing lens to reveal a dark little furball clinging to a branch eating a leaf. The sloths were so simple and elegant. Neither ambitious, nor impatient. I imagined they were just savoring their existence. Amelia admired how they embrace a snuggly life, a super-chill existence, which might be why they are so popular at zoos. Amelia was in sloth heaven.

The race started late. The kayak next to one swimmer, an American doctor, proved too narrow for the hefty support paddler and promptly sank. In the first seven kilometers, I was already struggling due to opposing currents. Making it to the first checkpoint and buoy should have taken two hours, but it was stretching into four and a half. I'd estimated the whole race would take six hours. At this pace, though, it would take 12, maybe up to 15 hours. I wasn't prepared for that kind of punishment. I hadn't trained for that distance, plus the jellyfish were bringing me down. Their stings were like little razors in the water, and you couldn't see them until they were wrapped around your face and neck. For such thin—nearly invisible!—silica threads, they sure packed a punch. The time had come for some serious soul-searching.

I was exhausted at 8 kilometers and still had 13 kilometers to go. We took stock of the situation. "Maybe I should get out?" I wondered aloud. Jafet said, "Let's go another feeding and see how you feel and where we are."

Just keep swimming.

Swimming Golfo Dulce

We had been feeding every 30 minutes with small bites of a few gels, but it was time to amp it up. Jafet fed me slices of fresh pineapple and mango, a corner of a protein bar, Stingers, and a lot of electrolytes. Turning to my mental conditioning techniques, I got back into the game. I put my head down and swam, visualizing Amelia waiting for me on the other side.

At 10 kilometers, the water in the middle of the Golfo Dulce turned as smooth as a swimming pool. Jafet's persistence was paying off.

As I swam on, I thought of the pure joy on Amelia's face when she saw her first sloth high up in a tree a few days earlier. "Ohhhh...!" She just stood there, mouth agape. We had talked about what that moment would be like for so long, and there it was. Then a family of endangered titi monkeys came leaping by on the canopy that surrounded us.

My mind was as blue as the Golfo Dulce. The jellyfish had mercifully disappeared, so I just relaxed into my stroke. I focused on the beauty of the water. I stopped fighting and started smiling. I just kept swimming. Breathing every 3-5-7 strokes. Swimming like a butterfly. Free and easy. *Light as a feather.*

There are four tropical fjords in the world, and the Golfo Dulce is one of them. The waters are jade blue and clear and calm compared to the adjacent Pacific Ocean. The water has a fresh taste upfront, but it's pleasantly musky on the back end. Costa Rican ocean water is distinct for its rich afternotes of mangrove roots and rain forest floor. My palette sensed a little bit of lime and the saltiness of a margarita combined with overlays of coconut husk.

Not only is it home to the migrating endangered Pacific humpback whales and hammerhead sharks, it also has an extensive ecosystem of coral reefs. Coral reef systems are complex and diverse. Astonishingly, about one quarter of all ocean species depend on the life that teems around them. Coral reefs provide safety and food. For this richness and significance, coral reefs are sometimes referred to as the 'rainforests of the sea.' They are actually living sea creatures related to sea anemones. The stony coral build structures of calcium carbonate, and these structures then form tropical reefs.

Sadly, in the Golfo Dulce as elsewhere around the world, reefs are dying at a rapid rate. There are plenty of reasons, and most of them are anthropogenic (human-caused): pollution, sedimentation, coastal development, overfishing, etc. According to scientists, about one quarter of the world's coral reefs have been destroyed and three quarters of what remains is in serious danger. Those fractions grow every day, and it's estimated that 90% of the world's coral reefs will be in danger by 2030.

Since 2015, Joanie Kleypas, and her fellow scientists at NCAR in Boulder, have partnered with the University of Costa Rica and the National Institute of Learning and the Nicuesa Eco Lodge on the Gulfo Dulce to create coral nurseries. They grow coral in a laboratory and then transplant fragments of coral onto a scaffolding-type structure at a few locations in the Gulfo Dulce. After it takes root and grows, they move it from the 'coral nursery' to coral gardens. Researchers don't know if these specific underwater communities will survive with climate change.

Joanie Kleypas and her colleagues are experimenting with ways to produce climate-tolerant corals. Their team has been called a model for research into how to rebuild coral reefs around the world. I still hold out hope that, if given a chance, bodies of water can recover from human degradation and ecological disaster. The restoration brings to mind Lake Pontchartrain and how the lake was able to recover after a few simple changes like stopping agricultural runoff and dredging for shells on the bottom of the lake, both of which destroy the fragile lake ecology.

Suddenly, on the Gulfo Dulce I'm swimming past 16 kilometers and knocking on the door of 17K.

The Dalai Lama says the two most important words in any

language are "love" and "gratitude." As the pain and suffering accumulated, I thought of how much I love my family. I thought of how grateful I was to be in the beautiful water of the Golfo Dulce feeling its warm embrace. We passed the final red buoy at 20K, and Jafet laughed and whooped.

I could see Amelia and Adri clearly now at the finish. I recalled how Amelia talked about how someday she could come back to the Golfo Dulce to harvest coral or maybe teach English. She had undergone her own transformation in these wet jungles. Her birthday didn't seem like mere coincidence, it was an opening of horizons and relationships. This swim was for her.

No matter how much love and gratitude I felt in my head and my heart, the rest of my body was feeling the full effects of the swim now. Electric currents from the jellyfish stings pulsated through my nerves. Armpits and shoulders burned from chafing, and I had a severe sunburn on my lower back.

I reached the finish in 9 hours and 6 minutes. Third place—out of four finishers. After I crossed the finish buoys, Amelia jumped in the water and I hugged her under pouring rain.

On the Gulfo Dulce with Amelia Moseley and Jafet Montero

PART THREE

CHAPTER TWELVE

AGENCIES OF NATURE

"Walking to the taffrail, I was in time to make out, on the very edge of a darkness thrown by a towering black mass like the very gateway of Erebus—yes, I was in time to catch an evanescent glimpse of my white hat left behind to mark the spot where the secret sharer of my cabin and of my thoughts, as though he were my second self, had lowered himself into the water to take his punishment: a free man, a proud swimmer striking out for a new destiny."

– Joseph Conrad, The Secret Sharer

Major John Wesley Powell, once considered the Godfather of the West for exploring and mapping the canyons on his 1869 geographic expedition, went on to become the second director of the U.S. Geological Survey, the first director of the Bureau of Ethnology at the Smithsonian Institution, and the first head of the Department of the Interior, establishing the Bureau of Reclamation. He was a true hero of the times and a model of national service to the wounded nation following the Civil War.

In his exploration of what is now Canyonlands National Park, the submerged recess under Lake Powell that is Glen Canyon, and the Grand Canyon, Powell realized that over eons, a sea floor becomes a mountain range and that those same mountains will eventually be washed down and carried away bit by bit as sediment back to the sea. The average lifespan of a mountain range is about 60 million years. It rises up by way of volcanoes, earthquakes, and geologic contortions. For evidence of the sea–floor-to-summit process, just look to the seashells found on mountain ranges.

Of course, for millennia religion tried to explain them as proof of Noah's Flood, not as symbols of earth's constantly changing geology and topography.

If we could convert geologic time to a rate we're more familiar with, John McPhee writes in his book, *In Suspect Terrain*, "continents would crawl like amoebae, rivers arrive and disappear like rain streaks down an umbrella, lakes would go away like puddles after rain." Powell attributed authorship of the Colorado Plateau to "the agencies of nature." He determined that such spectacular places were created "not by extravagant and violent use of power, but by the slow agencies which may be observed generally throughout the world, still acting in the same slow, patient manner." On the geologic clock, one million years is just the blink of an eye. The reality is that erosion over time has formed these canyons like a child building castles in the sand.

Some rocks in the Grand Canyon are among the oldest on earth at nearly two billion years, a little less than half the age of earth. If we conceive of that age, roughly 4.5 billion years, as a calendar year, dinosaurs would show up just as the Christmas holidays were beginning and disappear on December 26th. *Homo sapiens* would show up just in time for the New Year's Eve party on December 31st. As the clock counts down to midnight, *10, 9, 8...* With three seconds to go, the New World is discovered by Spain. The deep ruts that the Green and Colorado Rivers, over millions and millions of years, have carved into the earth give a good sense of just how small our place in it really is. From Gilgamesh to Ecclesiastes, Shelley's "Ozymandias" to today's finest poets, human ephemerality has inspired literature like few other subjects. Not to be outdone, Shakespeare notes, "Water drops have worn the stones of Troy,/ and blind oblivion swallowed cities up."

Our time on earth is simply too brief (and perhaps our mental capacity too limited) to fully grasp evolutionary changes. My limited exposure to water around the world, however, has given me a glimpse into them. Tasting the sediment of the Green River as it meticulously carves a path through the crust of the earth, I realize I'm just another infinitesimal particle bobbing along in the flotsam.

I recall that conversation at the confluence with friends one night about how acknowledging you're doomed brings a certain liberation. Canyonlands and the Grand Canyon, in particular, reveal the sweeping scale of time. Swimming through the canyons conjures a certain humility. Perhaps we aren't as important and precious as we think we are? Just another firefly. We are but a brief bioluminescence in the vast darkness of the night sea.

When the Powell expedition reached this point at the confluence, they could hear the tempest of the rapids of Cataract Canyon ahead and had no idea how much farther they could go. From the roar, they could have imagined thousand-foot falls. How tough and hardy those souls must have been, their clothes disintegrating until they were rags. Only the thinnest and coarsest of blankets kept them warm at night. They didn't have sunscreen and high-tech sun shirts or cans of propane to cook dinner and heat morning coffee (coffee was one of the few things they did have in abundance). No park rangers checked on their safety, no shuttle service moved their cars—no cars! No ice, no exit strategy. Blistering heat all day, biting cold all night. Their options were essentially to make it to the end or die. Exceedingly courageous, these adventurers seemed to be driven by an extreme sense of duty to the greater task and by their deep respect, if not always deep affection, for Major Powell.

* * * * *

My parents were raised in Northern Louisiana by Protestants and Scottish immigrants who had moved South chasing the oil boom. We were not Cajuns by blood. Thus, growing up in Lafayette, Louisiana, I thought of myself as an outsider. That I was adopted may have contributed to this sense of otherness. Even so, I spent my boyhood in the heart of Cajun country, a wild and mysterious place where the French Acadians settled following their expulsion from

Nova Scotia by the British for their Catholic beliefs.

They traveled down the Eastern Seaboard, and, at most points, were told to keep going. They circled Key West and made their way along the Gulf Coast, past New Orleans. Up the Mississippi River to Baton Rouge, then west into swamp, where they established a home in the marshlands. Lafayette became their capital, and the word, *Acadian*, morphed into *Cajun.* Incidentally, the Acadian diaspora serves as the background of Henry Wadsworth Longfellow's classic poem, *Evangeline*.

In a toast at our wedding in Telluride, Kristin's father, Clyde Howse, told how their family were also descendents from Acadia in Nova Scotia. He spoke of our marriage being perhaps a reunion of those who had fled Nova Scotia and New Brunswick for various points south, including Louisiana and northern Michigan. Our wedding represented a scattered culture coming full circle.

Today, some of the descendants of the original Acadians still live on small houseboats or in cabins on stilts in the bayous among cypress trees draped with Spanish moss. I'd say it's impossible to conceive of Cajun culture in South Louisiana without relation to the viscous, opaque water from which so much of it sprang. The bayou is where *aqua* meets *terra firma*, where steam rises off the swamp and collects in miasma. As rich in cultural traditions as it is in biological diversity. Blue herons, speckled trout, pelicans, and alligator snapping turtles are just a few of the species that signify home to me. And this is why I wanted to swim Lake Pontchartrain.

It's not easy living. A person should be afraid of the water in the Atchafalaya basin, where the Mississippi River Delta melts into the Gulf of Mexico, the largest swamp in the United States. Somehow the Cajuns didn't just survive here, they thrived. Like their ancestors, they are hardy people, survivors who live as capably on water as they do on land. And they'll be faced with more challenges to come. At this point, the Army Corps of Engineers' grand plan to harness the Mississippi River by creating levees has washed away precious alluvial soil. The lack of flooding is compromising the very existence of the marsh, which yields more and more to the waters of the Gulf of Mexico every year, making south Louisiana more susceptible to hurricanes.

Cajun culture also has a certain *joie de vivre.* They love life and have developed a unique culture in swamp country. In big pots and kettles over a fire, they created gumbo, jambalaya, red beans and rice, and other delicacies. Cajuns hunt and trap. Boil crabs and crawfish. Eat alligator *sauce piquante.* Fried catfish. Shrimp *etouffee*. Fresh crabs. These are the dishes of my childhood.

Beautiful music from handcrafted instruments has emerged from the bayous for centuries. When I think of the music of my childhood, I hear a lovely Cajun waltz played by the band, Beau Soleil, whose members lived just down the street from our family home, *Ti Frere's House.* And I recall the legend about how Coco Robicheaux, who hailed from Carencro, in Lafayette Parish, learned to play on an old guitar he'd strung with fishing line. Our neighbors spoke *Cajun French* or *French Acadien,* which is a music unto itself. While my last name was not Boudreaux, Thibodeaux, or Arceneaux, the bayous of Louisiana, full of Cajun music, Zydeco, *fais do-dos,* and "Ça c'est bons," were still a wonderfully wild place to grow up.

I could have never imagined then that Utah and the vast expanse of Canyonlands, places not even on my radar until I moved to Telluride in my mid-20s, would capture my fascination as they have.

* * * * *

The afternoon zephyrs begin to whip around as the day fades and the earth releases her heat. As the Green River swim progresses and the cold begins to seep in and the Zen-like trance starts to yield to discomfort, as always happens, there comes a reckoning. *Time to toughen up.* Sometimes I think of how I could be more durable—in the water, as a person, in my career. Resiliency and sustainability seem to be more fashionable terms these days, particularly among city planners and the like, but I'm referring specifically to *Adaptability.* Adjusting to changing circumstances. Dealing with the toll of everyday existence. Managing the difficulty of life in a constantly evolving world. I've come to realize that the innately human ability to adjust to fluctuating, even unpredictable, circumstances is yet another agency of nature.

* * * * *

I live in Boulder now, but New Orleans has always been my Soul City. The place where I was born and first came into my own after college working at Commander's Palace. When the city was battered by Hurricane Katrina in 2005, the hardiness of New Orleanians came to the fore as they rebuilt from the devastation. Across the city, scribblings began to appear. *Soul is Waterproof.* No hurricane was going to destroy this place. Not yet anyway. New Orleanians and the people of South Louisiana have grit and determination that will not be washed away. Their adaptability inspires me. We may need to learn a thing or two from Cajuns, who live where there is too much water. Just as we must remember the ancestral Puebloans, who tried to hold on where there was too little.

CHAPTER THIRTEEN

WATER AND WORDS

Cushion me soft, rock me in billowy drowse
Dash me with amorous wet - (the solitude of the swimmer)
When I wandered along over the beach, and undressing, bathed
Laughing with the waters
While they discuss I am silent, and go bathe and admire myself
Long enough have you dreamed contemptible dreams
Or have you timidly waded holding a plank by the shore
Now I will you to be a bold swimmer

– Walt Whitman, Song of Myself: Part 22

Staring at the blank page is akin to peering into the ocean's abyss. For better or worse, anything is possible.

"Swimming is the writer's sport, because it is the sport most like writing," claims writer Hanya Yanagihara. "To swim, as to write, is to choose an intense state of socially acceptable aloneness." For extroverts, writing and swimming are about the loneliest endeavors possible. I've often thought of writing a book as endurance swimming for the mind. Yanagihara says, "Swimming in the ocean is writing a novel; swimming in a pond is writing in a diary." I understand where she is coming from. For me, both entail a process that forces you to make decisions about who you are.

Our identity is based, in large part, on how we spend our limited time. In our daily life, do we make space for what's truly important? What is our purpose? What level of discomfort are we willing to accept in its pursuit? Writing forces us to define who we are through the stories and words we choose. Long distance swimming, perhaps even more austere, asks only, *Are you going to make it?* Your answer to that question (both the *if* and the *how*) will help you answer the staring-at-yourself-in-the-mirror-late-at-night question that both writing and swimming ultimately pose: *Who are you?*

It's not the pursuit of happiness, but the pursuit of purpose.

While there are significant rewards to them, both swimming and writing require paying your dues. I walked out of a swim practice one day with world-renowned astrophysicist and author Jeff Bennett as we spoke about swimming and writing. I listened closely when he said to me, "You've got to sit down and write even if you know it sucks." Whether it's swimming or writing, he explained, "You've got to get in the water, or sit your butt in the chair, and put your fingers on the keyboard... every day." He spoke about how writing was not waiting for the perfect moment or for inspiration to strike, but doing the work in spite of it. Like showing up for swim practice when you don't feel so hot. "This is the mark of a true professional," he said. "Doing the work not because it feels good, but because one must—even when it doesn't feel good. Even when it hurts."

The mental work in writing and swimming are similar. Strokes, like sentences, can be effortless or they can be difficult, depending upon the circumstances. Swimming and writing are both based on momentum—forward motion of the stroke and propulsion of the story. Both are ways for a person to make sense of the world by taking a step back to assess and by getting more involved. Simultaneously detaching from and digging in—another contradiction.

Yanigahara touches on this when she mentions feeling both inside and outside of herself while writing or swimming. She writes,"If you are an open-water swimmer, the sport also demands a particular kind of mental discipline, one in which you must simultaneously indulge your imagination while also asserting control over it." I felt that same paradox when I stepped off terra firma at the beginning of the Green River swim.

I think of two fundamental elements of writing—diction, and syntax—as analogous to the course and flow of a river. Like every stroke, every word follows a direction, building upon itself to form an arc (or narrative). The swirl of a dynamic sentence. An eddyline of ideas and possibilities. The thalweg of a story. In writing, as in swimming, we may know the course—the outline—but that which gets us there (words or strokes) materialize only in the consequent action of the moment.

Both writing and swimming demand the development of fitness and capacity. Training and building the right physical and mental muscles require a certain discipline. At least, they should. People usually only see the big swim or race. No one sees all the early morning practices. In writing, people only read the finished product, not the innumerable drafts upon drafts. The living of it. The upshot is that with writing, as with swimming, one only gets better with practice.

That advice about swimming from the core applies to writing as well. *Write from the belly.* Writing can be a full-body experience for me, engaging the head, heart, and core. Sometimes after a long bout of writing, I'm exhausted. My mind goes numb, and I'm physically worn out. I use a different take on my mantra to visualize myself in the act. *Write as a feather.* Where the writing pours out like quicksilver. Where words seem to float along with the currents.

THE BYRONIC TRADITION

Once I wondered if, in the end, we're merely the summation of the sentences we write. And then I realized I borrowed the notion from my swimming life. I tend to think that every body of water, everywhere I've swum, lives inside me. The molecules that have traveled around the world countless times and now reside within me will soon flow back to the depths of the oceans. I often think of all the water and words that have both inspired and challenged me. To me, they feel like elemental forces that capture attention even as they illuminate the way, like the torch Lord Byron carried on his swim through the Venice canals—or the sheaf of papers (some say his *Gallic Commentaries*) that Caesar held above the waterline as he swam from the attacking Egyptians.

Many of the great poets of the Romantic period infused this love of water and adventure and the sense of purification into their work. In fact, *esprit de Byron* was an essential part of the Romantic movement. He had a profound impact on the zeitgeist of his day, not merely through his words, which have outlived generations, but also through his lifestyle and adventures, which transcended words.

Even after writing his great works, such as *Don Juan*, he still considered swimming the Hellespont his greatest achievement; it was the one he spoke about most. It was as if the swim defined him, which then enabled him to bring forth such magnificent wordsmithing. It wasn't just the words of the Romantics, but also how they imbued their lives with the brightest colors.

"I fall upon the thorns of life! I bleed!" wrote Shelley.

Lord Byron's contemporary, Algernon Charles Swinburne, fellow poet, playwright, novelist, and social critic, loved to swim through rough seas and had a taste for "sea foam and the frothing of blood." The Romantics took on the new age by living their lives to the fullest. Shucking traditions and mores, they set up a template for life that influenced so much of progressive thought.

One of Byron's admirers was the great Russian poet and founder of modern Russian literature, Alexander Pushkin. His obsession with Byron began in his youth in St. Petersburg. As Charles Sprawson notes, "In the middle of winter, Pushkin would rise early, run down to the river, "break the ice with his fist and plunge into the freezing water."

Another devotee of Lord Byron, Edgar Allen Poe swam six miles up the James River, battling the current the whole way, when he was 15. Poe, like his hero, expressed more pride about his endurance swimming than he did any of his literary works.

Sprawson associates Poe with water, "the element towards which he was oriented, that polarised his imagination—the dark lake whose waters closed over the house of Usher, the fatal well below the pendulum, the descent into the Maelstrom."

Henry David Thoreau spent two years living (and writing) on Walden Pond, where swimming was part of his daily regimen. In the early mornings, he would walk the short distance from his cabin door to a little beach of gravel and dive in naked. The spot became known as Thoreau's Point. He considered swimming "a religious exercise, and one of the best things I did."

While writing *Zorba the Greek*, one of my favorite books, under Nazi Occupation, Niko Kazantzakis, wrote in the morning, then swam in the ocean, lunched, and in the afternoon rested during a siesta with some more writing at night. (Very much like the daily routine I aspire to.)

Water has acted as a lubricant for creativity throughout the ages. Walt Whitman maintained his verse took inspiration from the "soothing rustle" of the surf on the beaches of Long Island. He gave way to the seductiveness of the sea. He once wrote of being "carried along, as it were, like some expert swimmer, who has tired himself, and to rest his limbs, allows them to float drowsily and unresistingly on the bosom of the sunny river."

The connection of these great writers to the Byronic Tradition, their relationship to water and the surreal and natural world, is too transparent to deny. They dispensed with logic and the rigid scientific inquiry of the day and turned towards creativity. They turned away from the formal, clinical mindset of the early eighteenth century and toward a more candid expression of spontaneous feelings. They found comparisons to nature in their own lives and emotions, which they explored through poetry and words. These were no armchair poets and philosophers. In Byronic fashion, they got out there and did things. They jumped into the deep end.

Lord Byron's exploits and his influence on Webb would transform England into a modern swimming powerhouse in the 19th century. According to Sprawson, in the harbors of coastal towns, natural amphitheaters, thousands of spectators would gather to watch swimming contests through and beyond the breakers. London, in particular, gained a reputation as a mecca for swimmers. It boasted six permanent pools and seasonal floating baths stationed at various points along the Thames. It is no surprise that in Byron and Webb's century, with a little help from Benjamin Franklin, the English were widely regarded as the world's finest swimmers.

* * * * *

Memories keep flooding in. I chuckle recollecting David Amram composing jazz for nearly 15 hours on a party barge while I swam Pontchartrain, the notes he played connecting us to Jack Kerouac, Neal Cassady, and Allen Ginsberg. To Leander and Hero. To Franklin and Webb. To Annette Kellerman, Lynne Cox and Sarah Thomas. And to our standard torchbearer, Lord Byron. I think about swimming with a torch, and then I start laughing. Not at that. At the thought of Leander getting lost in the storm while swimming to his lover, Hero... It's not funny at all—it's tragic! But I'm getting pretty loopy, you see. I've been in the water for over 14 hours now.

Time and light stretch until they both seem to stand still and speed up simultaneously. This tiny speck of time in the grand scheme of things seems to me to last forever. Cold water, hot sun. Meaning, chaos. Separately and together. Contradictions resolve themselves and melt away in the current.

CHAPTER FOURTEEN

RACING AGAINST SUNLIGHT

Amid the mixed-up, delirious Green River gumbo of random thoughts concerning authors, poets, musicians, and other assorted characters, I return time and again to my mantra. Light as a feather. *Light* on the inhale. *As a feather* on the exhale. After a feeding somewhere around mile 38, I swing my arms back into what feels like endless rotation. Besides the deep chill working itself into my bones, a sludge has started to cover my brain. I try to repeat my mantra, but the words, simple as they are, don't come. It's shocking. That which has sustained me for so long has now deserted me.

Feathers and...

I rummage around for any of the other go-to phrases I've trained with over the years, but none materialize.

Cool as a...

Love and...

After months of recitation, after daily visualization and repetition, my tether seems to have frayed. As in every swim, there comes a time of reconciliation. When the situation becomes so soul-crushing, the question of *Why*? seems like a bad joke you've played on yourself. Plus, my shoulder feels like it's about to give out.

After the sandbar at mile 18, the river hasn't regained its push. We've gone from 3.3 mph at the beginning to more like 2.5 mph or slower. At mile 28, I thought we should have been at 31. As we move deeper into Canyonlands, the flows keep getting slower, not faster as they usually would. At times, the river was ankle-deep. According to calculations, a consistent 3 mph would've put us at the confluence in 17.5 hours, around 10:00 p.m. With 12 miles to go, it becomes evident we won't arrive at the confluence until after 2:00 a.m.

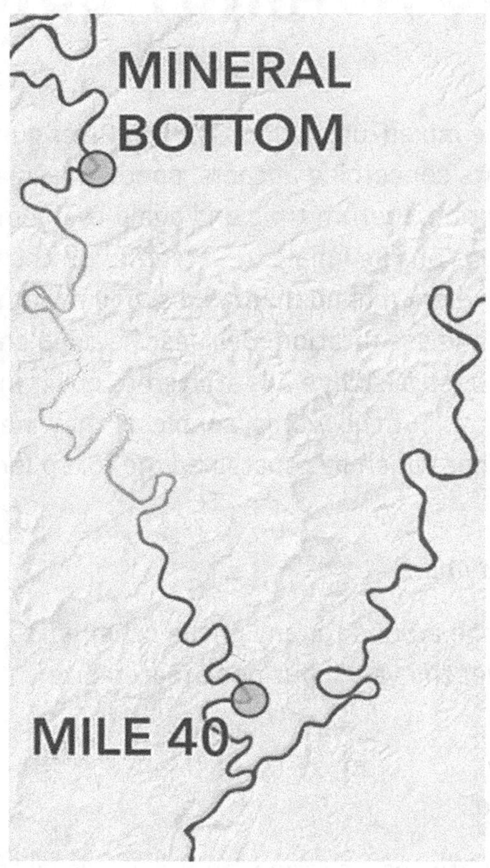

Mineral Bottom to MIle 40

Meanwhile the sun is setting and the temperature is dropping by the minute. We're running out of light and time.

Even as reality demands to be reckoned with, my vision of standing up in triumph at the confluence refuses to fade. Despite the raging intercostal muscle, I'm ready to keep going and swim into the night. But in the backbeat of these twilight strokes, I remember our *Safety Plan* and know we're bumping up against it.

We'd agreed that if it became clear we wouldn't make it

to the confluence until after 10 p.m., we would need to terminate the swim.

That was *The Safety Plan*, and I certainly don't want to put the team in danger amid rocks, sand bars, and our worst nemesis, impalement.

I think of all of this and more, and the choice becomes clear. At that moment, I know what I must do. With the evening light dripping down the sandstone walls the deep hue of blood agate, my feet touch the bottom of the river and I stand up. I do the unimaginable.

Never in my life have I exited a swim. Through storms and getting lost. Through lightning, alligators, and sickness. My support boat capsizing. Running headfirst into a snake. I've crapped on myself and swum over my own vomit. I've never stopped. Never.

"I know there are some realities setting in," I say as I lift my goggles. "I don't want to give up." But I have to. The time has come to pull the plug. I stop swimming.

Between themselves, I learn later, Fiebig and Mark have been having hushed exchanges about an exit strategy. To their credit, they have been waiting for me to make the decision myself.

Mike points to a small rock outcropping on river right. I swim over, trudge through a muddy hole, and crawl onto the rock. Standing is too unsteady, so I sit there for a moment. My hands cover my face and disappointment sweeps through me. I'm bone-tired. Emotionally spent. All feeling is burned out of me, except for the hot coals of regret. Fiebig comes up and puts his arms around me.

"I don't want to let anybody down," I tell him, shoulders heaving, tears streaming down my cheeks.

"You didn't," he assures me.

All the planning, preparation, and dreaming that have led

up to this moment seem to evaporate quicker than the daylight. A profound sadness creeps in.

Exiting the Green River Swim

Warming up after Green River Swim

Hugging Mike Fiebig

Not for me. Not for our swim. I've trained the best way I knew how. Assembled the very best team. I've swum 40 miles in 14 hours and 36 minutes. But not to the 52-mile goal. Not to the Confluence. I didn't grasp the brass ring. Our planning has accounted for just about every contingency, but there's one we couldn't have prepared for.

The F Word: *Flows.*

No, I'm hurting for the river. With the lowest flows on record, the volume of water in the river is about an eighth of what it should be.

As I put on warm clothes and climb into the front seat of the two-person kayak with Mark, blackness has already descended upon the canyon like a thick, wet blanket. My body shivers to warm up. There are no stars or moon. Over the next hour, Mark paddles mostly in silence, the canyons sheathed in squid ink. We switch on our Nite Ize lights, but that only gives us visibility about 10 to 15 feet out. Mark tracks off Fiebig and the *Lagniappe*. John Mans is now using lights for his camera on the bow of the canoe for direction. This swim started out as a celebration of the Green River. Now it feels more like a funeral cortege moving along the water.

In the boat after Green River

It's been quiet most of the past three hours, but as we pass a camp on the left, three people emerge out of nowhere with flashlights beaming on bare backsides. Here we are weaving through a silent river and we get *mooned!* The big white butts juxtaposed against the towering cliffs and their tents send us all into laughter. The sheer absurdity shifts the mood. We paddle on through the night. After eating and rehydrating, I start to feel better about what's transpired.

After paddling for nearly three and a half hours, which would be a good effort in and of itself, we turn the corner at Mile One to where the Green River meets the Colorado River. Colored lights illuminate our crew waiting on the beach. With winds whipping around, we pull into the confluence shortly before 11:00 p.m.

All told, Fiebig's GPS watch has recorded nearly 28,000 paddle strokes over 18 hours.

Earlier, paddling in the darkness, I'd asked Fiebig if he would explain to the group how it had ended. I didn't feel up to the task of putting it into words. Fiebig thought about it for a moment and then said he thought that ultimately it was my story to tell. He was right. Somewhere along that dark paddle, something settled within me. I'm not sure if it was the physical distance we'd made from the exit-point or the time that had elapsed, but I started to gain perspective. Regret began to yield to acceptance as I realized there wasn't anything I could have done differently.

Our journey had become a much different story, one about the flows of the river and rivers throughout the West.

By the time we pull in and get out of the boats and everyone greets us with hugs all around—two extra-long ones for Charlie and Kristin—I'm actually looking forward to telling everyone about our big day.

Hugging Kristin and Charlie at the confluence

I explain what went down. How I gave it my best shot. How my knuckles are raw from scraping against the bottom so many times. I demonstrate how sometimes it was easier to crawl than to stand up. I do a little dance to demonstrate how in water no more than a foot deep, I'd have to bring my legs forward like a frog, swimming like the early English.

Demonstrating swimming like a frog

The team is in a mood to celebrate what I have done, not lament what I haven't. Matt Rice says, "It was hard enough to paddle down the river. We can't believe you swam it!" They're well-acquainted with the low flows after having to get out and drag the rafts across shallow water at various points.

This swim wasn't a race. There weren't any medals or prize money to be won, but there were stakes involved. Here at the confluence my feelings are still raw, and I know everyone can sense it. Perhaps for that very reason, talking about it feels so cathartic. It's part of processing what I've just been through. Of course, I'm disappointed about not reaching my goal, but that's the risk we take when we set up these kinds of endeavors. Like swimming to the wrong island. Like losing your support boat in the night. As in life, we can't take things for granted or cling too tightly to expectations. Right now, laughing and talking with the team is just what I need.

Nite Ize lights at the confluence

Past midnight now, with the wind whipping, we sit around colored LED lanterns, eat burritos, and drink a little chardonnay out of a box. I crawl into the tent, and Kristin rubs my throbbing shoulder. The river's current continues to swirl within me. Adrenaline courses through my veins.

As I lie on the sand, I feel as if I'm still floating, still riding away on the water whispering just beside us. As if I'm one of the figures from the Cave of Swimmers in Egypt 10,000 years ago. Part swimming, part rising up into the ether. Inside of me, something has died, and something else has been born. Sleep should come easily because I'm exhausted, but I toss and turn with the tent flapping in the wind. Just like the previous night at Mineral Bottom where we began, a lifetime ago.

CHAPTER FIFTEEN

RETURNING RAPIDS: RAFTING CATARACT CANYON

The highest good is like water.
Water gives life to ten thousand things and does not strive.
It flows in places men reject and so is like the Tao.

– *Lao Tzu, Tao Te Ching*

When the sun comes up after the Green River swim, we have good coffee and breakfast, and Fiebig and Mike Dehoff lead a team meeting about what to expect over the next four days of whitewater rafting. This day is going to be light and easy, though. We camp three miles downriver at the Brown Betty rapid, the historic start of Cataract Canyon and the roar of the whitewater comes alive. We pull over at a nice beach where we have the afternoon to just chill. Some of us paddleboard in the wake of the rapids, some of us settle in under a gnarled little cottonwood tree at the top end of the beach where there's shade. We read, talk, doze off, and revel in not doing much at all. The crew of five boats and 16 people has been on the move nonstop for several days now. Everyone enjoys a rest day.

We're going to need it. Now that the swim portion is over, the full team readies itself for the nearly 50 miles of Cataract Canyon, which may be the wildest stretch on the Colorado River. Most of the water from Colorado, Montana, and Utah converges in these rough-and-tumble rapids.

Mike Dehoff and Meg Flynn—collectively known as the Flyhoffs—are a part of the Returning Rapids Project. They were also along for part of the Fiebig's Source-to-Sea trip. Through Cataract Canyon, they show us old features of the Colorado River that are being revealed as Lake Powell recedes and the river reclaims itself. Since its inception, the man-made lake has reached far up Cataract Canyon and deposited an overwhelming amount of sediment that would have normally continued down the river. The Returning Rapids Project matches old photographs with what is coming back to life now that the sediment is washing away. The rapids that Major Powell ran are now reappearing.

This may be a small silver lining of *aridification*. As Elizabeth Kolbert points out in her 2021 *New Yorker* article about Returning Rapids, climate change catches her mid-sigh: "The wind-sculpted cliffs and sandstone arches... the grottoes, hanging gardens, and amphitheatres big enough for 'God's own symphony orchestra' described by Abbey—it seemed heartbreaking that all this was lost. The reservoir—Lake Foul, to its detractors—would, I assumed, last far longer than I would. There was no way I was going to get to see what lay beneath it.... It turns out I was wrong."

As Lake Powell recedes and shrinks, over 30 miles of river has been exposed. Among the more notable features of its ebbing are 150-foot high walls of sediment deposits where the river meets the lake. Before those original rapids can be uncovered, the river must cut through this sediment. It's an incredible amount of mud and muck, which should not have been here in the first place.

America's most prolific dam builder and Commissioner of the Bureau of Reclamation from 1959 to 1969, Floyd Dominy, built Glen Canyon dam and many others around the US. He infamously promised that sediment would never be a problem here. If Dominy wanted a legacy, he sure got one. Many river runners now refer to the obnoxious layer of mud sediment, which should be flowing all the way through Glen Canyon and creating the beaches of the Grand Canyon, as the "Dominy Fecal Formation."

* * * * *

For anyone, but especially for boaters and other river rats, Cataract Canyon is a hallowed place. A carved earthen cathedral of awe and wonder. Being with Matt Rice in Cataract Canyon, after a dozen years knowing each other and strategizing in the trenches of the water wars, is a special time indeed. He is another soul like Mark Williams, our friendship another channel that runs deep and swift. Matt Rice and I talk and laugh into the starry nights long after everyone else has said goodnight. *Howling at the moon!*

Without my *compañeros*, I couldn't survive the harshness of life. As we think about ways to not only survive, but also to thrive in a changing world, we need to remember that simply connecting with people might be the most important.

Matt Rice is another I trust with my life. More than most, he knows the problems we're having with water, but he prefers to talk about solutions. He is insistent that for the health of the overall planet and environment, we need to leave more water in the stream for fish and habitat. That means we have to use less water for agriculture, municipalities, and development. We can't just suck our rivers dry, dam them to high heaven, and then dump the runoff. It also means we have to be smarter about residential use—putting a stop to the construction of new subdivisions in the desert and sweeping, irrigated lawns.

The alarming news is that in the West we have already reached the point at which there is not enough water to go around.

THE LAW OF THE RIVER

The Colorado Compact, a document that defines much of the history and development of the American West, is remarkably stark and simple at a mere four pages. When you strip away the legalese and other fluff, there are only a few paragraphs that outline the terms of delivery and amounts of water for the past 100 years between the Upper Basin (Colorado, Utah, New Mexico, and Wyoming) and the Lower Basin (Arizona, Nevada, and California.) The document, and accompanying agreements, is known as the Law of the River.

What is happening to the Green River is a living, breathing example of what is happening to rivers all over the world. With climate change, there will be a few winners and a whole lot of losers. Some rivers in the wet northern hemisphere may flood uncontrollably—especially in the Pacific Northwest, where forest fires give way to mudslides.

The Mississippi River Basin also needs room to breathe, to overflow in the spring into the interior lands and natural barriers that protect terra firma and provide a foundation for flora and fauna. This natural flooding and receding is what creates the rich "Sportsman's Paradise" of the bayous, as touted on the Louisiana state license plate. Floods and fires constitute a cycle of disaster and creation—and always have.

The simple reality is that people can't live where fish can't swim. Water *is* the defining issue of our time. We have a responsibility to do a better job of protecting the lifeblood of the planet. The abiding lesson I have learned from swimming is simple: As the rivers, lakes, and oceans go, so do we. *We are the water.*

* * * * *

After our last dinner in Cataract Canyon, Mark asks us to gather round at the river's edge above the thundering Big Drop Three rapid to sprinkle his father-in-law's ashes into the river. He says a few kind words about the man, a good soul. He had grown up in the hills of Arkansas, where apparently his collection of guns was only outdone by his collection of tequila, from which Mark brought a fine bottle of Don Eduardo Triple Distilled Silver. After the touching remarks and a moment of silence, Mark sends the ashes fluttering out into the current as the rapids we'll be facing the next day thunder below.

As the ashes float down the river, Mark describes each cycle as a journey: life and death, birth, and rebirth. He compares it all to this very trip. This canyon. We pass the tequila around and make toasts.

That night, I feel particularly grateful for Mark's ubiquitous presence on these adventures. Zelig-like, he appears at life-changing moments. Political campaigns, long distance swims in the middle of the night, or simply walking down Pearl Street in Boulder. He's one of those characters who materialize on a Hero's Journey as the helper, protector, and guide.

Ingrained with his military training is a strong sense of commitment. If he accepts a mission, he sees it through. I know he always has my back, and this inspires me to live up to his support and investment. While our adventures are fun and we both laugh a lot, deep down we both know they are serious. These swims are not about me. They are about everyone who contributes time and energy along the way. They are about the stories that arise through them, passing from our time on the water to later recountings, such as this one. Mark doesn't mess around. That's what separates what I do now from the boondoggle days in the beginning. Not everyone believes in your dream, nor are they required to, but it sure is a blessing when people do.

Underneath the shaded cottonwood tree that lazy afternoon following the swim, I reflect on all I love. My friends. The possibility of doing these adventures at all. The water. My health. These canyons. My wife. My children, Charlie and Amelia. The eagles soaring overhead. The self-knowledge I've attained through the water. All the experiences that fill my jar.

Like the layers of sandstone and limestone that tell the history of the canyon walls, each swim lives within me as part of my own history. Sometimes these swims really do feel monumental. At other times, they feel rather ordinary—the Green River just another swim on another day. Whether it's on Pontchartrain or in the Caribbean, each swim is mostly just an opportunity to be in the water and have an adventure. I hope to keep swimming as long as I can. And as long as there are bodies of water to swim in. While I'm initially disappointed not to have reached the confluence, the whole journey has been deeply moving. The process of setting the goal, planning it with Matt Rice, working with my coach, Josiah Middaugh, following Mike Fiebig as he led the way. The discipline and fitness it has brought to my life. On the Green River Swim, we've forged lasting friendships and made connections that continue to ripple beyond the canyons.

As we rejoined the default world away from the river and the canyons, we came back to cell phone reception and said our goodbyes. Most river people don't like to compare trips to one another. Each trip embodies elements of good and bad. Your worst weather with no dinner may turn out to be one of your most memorable nights ever. When leaving the boat ramp at the North Wash take-out point, I felt that many of our crew were sincere when they said it was a particularly special river trip. One for the ages.

Six months later, American Rivers produced a short documentary called *Silent River* about the swim and the diminishing flows in Western waterways. As the co-chair of the Southwest Regional Board for American Rivers, I will continue to give voice to the entire basin of the Colorado River. At this point, I consider myself an Ambassador for Water. For me, it's about how I can use swimming to get people to think differently about life's most important resource. If we are to survive, there must be a stronger connection between people and water.

Sometimes that begins by simply getting in it.

CHAPTER SIXTEEN

THE SEA OF GALILEE

Ten months after the Green River swim, I'm standing on a little rocky clearing on the north shore of the Sea of Galilee with the moon arcing over the ancient city of Tiberius in Israel. A chill sweeps up my spine. The official observer, Anat Grossman, gives the word that the boat's ready and the swim can begin. As instructed, I put my hands over my head to signal I'm starting. I wade into the crisp water and start out at a brisk pace to warm up my body. I try to fathom that I'm actually here, skimming across the fine sheen of the Sea of Galilee in the moonlight. It's otherworldly and surreal, and I feel like I'm floating through it.

The taste of the water is hard to place. There are notes of bread and white linen. Perhaps what a wedding dress might taste like if you kissed it? Or maybe the bouquet of starched bed sheets from a hotel I once slept in. Then it hits me, the water of Galilee has the distinct flavor of the wafer I regularly received at communion growing up in the Episcopal Church. *The Bread of Christ*. Like the wafer, the water of Galilee tastes almost like nothing, which is what good water should taste like. Clean and crisp. A palate-cleanser for all senses and emotions.

As I swim past the twinkling lights of settlements and kibbutzim—one of which, on the left, is where ice swimmer Ram Barkai grew up—the first gilded rays of sunlight crowning the earth at twilight give the early morning a heavenly glow.

I first met Gad Reich in New Orleans in 2014 when he was attending Tulane Law School. Since then, he's been encouraging me to come visit his home in Tel Aviv. We started throwing around the idea of a swim on the Sea of Galilee (or Kinneret, as it's known in Israel). Thus another cycle begins.

The next thing you know, we're having a virtual meeting with Guy Cohen of the Galilee Marathon Swimming Association (GMSA). Tickets are booked, dates are set. GMSA arranges for a support boat and Anat for the swim of 20.6 km (about 12.5 miles).

Stas Schupek is assigned as my boat captain. He's a world champion wakeboarder and has sailed all over the world. When we meet the night before our swim, I can tell he has a calm, steady presence, as any good captain should. It sure didn't keep him from cranking the music, though. Stas kept the boat rocking with reggae, Euro beats, and good old-fashioned rock and roll. At one feeding, he blasted Led Zeppelin's "Kashmir" from the back speakers. *Yeah You Rite!*

As per usual, I can't hear what people are saying, but I'm present with the boat and I can sense the energy. Gad and Anat dance to the music in the morning sunlight and look like they're having fun. They make me smile. At feedings, they holler encouragement and keep the attitude light.

Just like the beat of the music, Stas keeps a very efficient line, guiding me by the nose of the boat off my right side exactly as we talked about the night before. He's cut from the same cloth as the others who've captained for me in the past: Mark Williams, Mike Fiebig, Mike Dehoff, Michael Feduccia, Allen Buras, and others. Boat people. From rivers to oceans to lakes, boat captains are a distinct breed. Like bass players in a band, they thrive by living in-the-pocket. A steady, assuring backbeat.

Behind me to the north rise snow-capped mountains and the source of the River Jordan. The lowest river in the world, it begins at the foot of Mount Hermon in Lebanon, where the Hasbani River and the Baniyas River from Syria meet. It's about 225 miles from where I begin the swim. Once the river crosses into Israel, it is joined by the Dan River. From there it flows into Galilee. There are many references to the River Jordan throughout Hebrew and Christian texts, including as the location of the baptism of Jesus. Many consider it to be one of the most sacred rivers in the world.

Galilee is the site of many of Jesus's teachings, including the Sermon on the Mount, and miracles, such as feeding the multitude, when he turned a few fish and loaves of bread into many. It is also written he walked on water here. In another of his most famous miracles, recounted in Mark 4:39-41, Jesus crosses the Sea of Galilee with his disciples. When a tempest arises on the water, "he arose, and rebuked the wind, and said unto the sea, '*Peace! Be still!*' And the wind ceased, and there was a great calm. And he said unto them, '*Why are ye so fearful? How is it that ye have no faith?*' And they feared exceedingly, and said to one another, 'What manner of man is this, that even the wind and the sea obey him?'"

Rembrandt captured the scene in a 1633 oil painting, *The Storm on the Sea of Galilee*. The painting shows a close-up view of Jesus and his disciples fighting against a raging storm in an attempt to control their fishing boat. Rembrandt majestically captures the tension as a huge wave overtakes the bow and the sail is ripped and tattered. One disciple is seen vomiting over the side while another, looking directly at the viewer, is a self-portrait of Rembrandt himself. While the disciples struggle, only Christ remains calm. It is the only known Rembrandt painting set on water.

A deep sense of history emanates from the water I stroke through. Fortunately, as the first rays of sun peak over the mountains, its surface is calm and glassy. We are starting early to avoid the legendary afternoon winds that whip up most days.

The heavy riff of *Kashmir* keeps us charging across.

CREATIVE WATER MANAGEMENT

Whatever its religious significance, the River Jordan, a hard-working little river if ever there was one, delivers water to this moderately sized lake, Galilee—not technically a *sea*—which, in turn, supplies critical fresh water to 9.2 million people in Israel. In the past, the Kinneret supplied about a quarter of Israel's water consumption, but following the drop in water levels as a result of years of drought, water pumping from the lake decreased and desalination plants became the main water supplier. Today, the Sea of Galilee provides between 2% and 13% of total consumption. These are geopolitically strategic bodies of water, central to world religions, and mired in war and conflict.

Israel is 60% desert. With limited supply and increasing demand, the country has had to be creative with water management. When the modern state of Israel was established in 1948, water planning was at the very heart of its foundation. Before it was a state, there were about 150,000 Jews living there and about 834,000 total inhabitants of Palestine. The British, who controlled the region, claimed there was no way it could support more than two million people in total. During World War II, when the British became preoccupied and stretched too thin, migration of the Jews to the land of Israel began in earnest. It was out of necessity that the Israelis developed more water.

That's when administrators got to work creating a plan called the *National Water Carrier.* Their key to national self-sufficiency included essentially creating pipes and water systems from the Kinneret in the north to multiple points south. They tracked every single drop of water inside or close to the boundaries of the proposed state of Israel. During this time, the Israelis turned to the Colorado River as a model for how it transported water through the desert to Southern California. They added sophisticated techniques such as collecting stormwater, recycling sewage for agricultural reuse, accessing deep aquifers with advanced technology, and other water-conserving measures.

Starting as a socialist state, Israel, with its cosmopolitan capital of Tel Aviv, quickly developed into a capitalist economic powerhouse of the Middle East. In an ironic twist, it was only able to make such a transition by way of a state-controlled, centrally planned approach to managing water. One may even go so far as to say that aggressive water development, technology advancements, and smart planning account for how modern Israel was founded in the first place.

Perhaps the most important thing I learned on my visit was that there is a key difference between the Israeli and the American approach to water: In Israel, water is the common property of all. Usage is managed for the greatest good. Just because you own land doesn't mean you have rights to the water on, under, or adjacent to it. In Israel, you don't even have rights to the water in the sink or toilet.

By contrast, in the U.S., one has personal property rights to water (this is my wife Kristin's specialty, water rights law). Ultimately, the approach to water is a cultural decision: *Which is more important, an entire community's well-being and sustainability or an individual's freedom and property? And how do the laws and usage reflect those values?*

* * * * *

At a conference for the Water Education Foundation in Santa Fe in 2022 commemorating the centennial of the Colorado Compact, I spoke about my Green River swim and our relationship with water. There was a reception at the Palace of the Governors on the historic Plaza, where the document had been signed. One hundred years later, the attendees represented a much wider demographic than did those who originally negotiated the protocols. This time, there were women, Tribal representatives, and environmental interests. The conference addressed a number of issues, but none bigger than the question: *Will the document created 100 years ago serve us for the next 100 years?*

I'll be honest: the prospects don't look great. The Compact was predicated on the assumption that there was much more water to go around. With climate change, that assumption no longer holds. There is simply a lot less water in the stream, and that's why the bathtub rings of Lake Powell and Lake Mead keep growing—but we keep on using just as much or even more. Just as much water continues to be pumped to the thirsty Front Range of Colorado through transmountain diversions despite decreasing flows. There will be tough questions, painful decisions, and big sacrifices regarding who gets the remaining water. For instance, one group might think it's a no-brainer to curtail water to California, which they may perceive as the biggest water hog. And another group agrees that it really is brainless since the Imperial Valley provides the entire United States with 90% of its winter fruits and vegetables. Because of the "use it or lose it" doctrine embedded in the Law of the River, farmers, ranchers, and all other users are incentivized to use up every drop of the river. However, of the entire flows of the Colorado River, about 80% are used for agriculture throughout the lower basin and much of it is just plain hay. Alfalfa and grass.

Israel learned a thing or two from the western United States, and now we may want to take a few lessons from them. I believe we have to shift our mindset. I'm not entirely dismissing Western libertarian values, but in the case of our changing climate, the 'Law of the River' may not be adequate to meet the challenge.

And the stakes couldn't be higher. The scarcity of water in the American West and around the world will affect nearly everyone, directly or indirectly, not just in the drop of local water levels, but in the availability of food, energy, clean drinking water, and other resources necessary for the modern world to function as it does.

* * * * *

As I swim under the twinkling stars on Galilee, I do feel a little of the magic of the place. The water is beautiful. Crystal and crisp. As the weather heats up and the fresh spring runoff diminishes, however, the flows slow down and the water becomes turbid. The Jordan and Kinneret face the same challenges as do all other fresh water sources around the world, especially those located in a desert, such as the Green River and the Colorado River. The swim is a good challenge, and further confirmation of just how fragile our water systems really are.

Yes, Galilee is where Jesus declared it was the meek who shall inherit the earth. In another light, it's just a lake. Swimming across the Sea of Galilee is another beautiful and fortuitous swim, but it doesn't differ all that much from most other bodies of freshwater around the world. It is overworked, over-appropriated, and underappreciated.

Entering the most southern end near the finish, where Galilee slowly flows back into the River Jordan, the water turns chalky with water grasses and has a slimy texture. Trudging up the steps of a landing on the south end of the Kinneret, I raise my arms over my head, just as in the finish of nearly every other swim. I've successfully completed the 20.6 kilometer swim in 7 hours and 24 minutes to become the 38th person in history and the 6th American to swim the length of the Sea of Galilee.

PARTING THE RED SEA

After the swim, we speed back to Tel Aviv, rest, and enjoy a good dinner. Gad has organized a party with family and friends at a club where we celebrate late into the night.

The day after the swim and the party, we sleep in and walk around the ancient port city of Jaffa, where Gad lives. That afternoon, I attend my first Passover celebration at a house on the hills overlooking Jerusalem on one side and Tel Aviv on the other. I discover that the host, Arieh O'Sullivan, is an Irish Jew who grew up in South Louisiana, *of all places*. He's also a journalist, and we become fast friends.

After the dinner and a long night of singing, eating, and storytelling, we leave at 2:30 a.m. for Eilat, the border crossing of

Israel and Egypt. A group of eight of us are headed to Sinai.

The five-and-a-half-hour border crossing in the early morning proves to be almost as difficult as the swim across Galilee. Deep fatigue seeps in with the heat. The final 'payment' of *baksheesh* at the last checkpoint is made, and soon we're bumping along in the back of a little pickup truck. For hours and hours, we ride across the desolate Sinai desert, battered and windblown. The occasional withered camel doesn't even bother lifting its head as we pass by. At least, we're seated on cushions.

I've wrapped my trusty old peacock-imprinted sarong around my head and face. Throughout the years, this simple cloth, more than just the traditional wrap around the waist, has served as a scarf, table cloth, towel, sun shade, beach blanket, and as fashionable dinner wear when paired with a tuxedo jacket, among myriad other uses. When picking among survival items, the sarong is one of the most useful in my opinion—depending upon your taste and style.

As the truck takes a sweeping left turn through a broad opening in the canyon, the glistening Red Sea reveals itself: turquoise water set against a stark and unforgiving desert with nary a speck of vegetation.

We finally find ourselves at the edge of nowhere.

On the Blue Lagoon of the Red Sea, we camp with a family of Bedouins and are given a 'Hoosha,' a little hut with a mattress and no running water or electricity. Talk about hardy, tough people! The Bedouins have lived here in the desert of the Sinai and throughout the Middle East as nomads for millenia. I wonder if they're so considerate and hospitable *despite* their survival in a place so inhospitable or because of it. I think they understand how fragile life is. They've created an austere way of life adapted to the harsh environment. The Bedouins remind me a little of the Cajuns, except that their struggle is the reverse: a dearth of water instead of a deluge.

For five glorious days, we live on the beach, completely disconnected. No more traveling or planning or worrying or perseverating. Some go snorkeling; the real life here is under the water on the coral reefs. I enjoy a gentle morning swim out to a reef to get the kinks worked out.

The Red Sea has the effervescence of a nice prosecco but made of seashells. Similar to tequila, but instead of salt, the fluted rim would be dipped in the exquisitely ground dust of ancient mollusks, sea creatures, and blasted desert rock.

We lie around all afternoon under the thatched roof of a hut. Some break out water colors and paint landscapes, others play guitar, read books, and journal. There's a sense that one long journey has come to an end and another is just beginning. Like the parting of the Red Sea, the distant shore has come into view, and now I've finally *arrived.*

As we all admire an extended blush-rose sunset, I lay back in repose, grab a palmful of sand, and let the grains pour out between my fingers. I think of my experiences and journeys and all the challenges and difficulties I've faced over the years—how formidable they seemed in the moment, how quickly they ended up sliding into the past. The granules sift through, leaving behind pebbles and flakes, and I think of all the friends who have supported me along my way. I set them aside in another little pile.

Coming night paints this silent, sandy desert an unnameable shade of barely blue. I'm reminded of Lake Tahoe, a blue incapable of being recreated on any paint store palette. A crystal azure that extends to seemingly endless depths, but is also right there in your face.

In the gloaming, I separate broken shells from sand by touch. These, I decide, stand for lessons I've learned along the way. This scalloped semi-disc is for building a team and keeping it together; this one with a hole in it is for all the training; a vulva-shaped fossil represents all the visualization along the way—not just envisioned goals, but obstacles I envision overcoming.

Others may have different values and priorities, but for me, I choose to keep charging forward. I will keep chasing moments like swimming the Green River, Pontchartrain, the Caribbean, Costa Rica, Galilee, like spending time with friends on this remote beach in Sinai. I do fear what climate change is doing to our planet, but I'm not scared enough to give up living life. I know we can adapt.

This is what my DNA tells me, anyway. The feeling deep in my gut.

The sun sets over the mountains, the sky turns the color of poached salmon, and on a long slow exhale, I let go.

Like the sand falling from my hand, all the planning, traveling, training, and all the stress dissolves into the Red Sea lapping at my feet.

I wonder if I came all this way, swam every stroke, for this moment right here. But then I know, under that dazzling Egyptian sky, that I haven't arrived at all. Hardly.

Other waters already call.

"Green River" by Phil Lewis

GO WHERE GROTTOS ECHO

Let us go where the path is forward
Never straight
Where secret jungles beckon
Howler monkeys screech
Waterfalls roar

Bath naked in a high mountain pond
Gaze upon places of wonder and transcendent beauty
Appearing at first as nothingness and Godforsaken

Become gloriously lost
Tired and lonely
Dusty and desicate

Go where ravens call
Thunder strikes
Where grottos echo

Hear streams sing a purling lullaby
Glimpse the tracks of the Snow Leopard
Traipse through miasmal swamps
Feel the crunch of toes on the evening sand

Make yourself laugh

Around a mysterious canyon wall
Treasure awaits
Wealth not measured in gold
Stories not yet told
Never too old

Say hello to your fears
Then Goodbye

You are the person you've been waiting for

GREEN RIVER SWIM LOG

The swim was ratified by the governing body of WOWSA as the first of its kind and the longest swim ever on the Green River for 40 miles in 14 hours and 36 minutes.

Green River Swim Observer's Log

Sunday, June 27, 2021

As recorded by Mike Fiebig

For World Open Water Swimming Association

We pushed off from Mineral Bottom at 4:58 AM on July 27, 2021, at mile marker 52 on the Stillwater Canyon section of the Green River. Water temps went from approx. 71° to 76° F that day. Air temps were 65° to 95° F. The river was flowing at approximately 1800-2000 cfs. These stats can be found at the Green River (town) USGS gauge, 45 miles upstream of where we put in, which is why these are "approximate" temps and flows and not exact. There are a couple of irrigation diversions and small tributaries between the Green River gage and Mineral Bottom. The significant pulse of water that started showing up down at the Confluence on July 28 and 29 had not yet reached us on the swim day. One can see that the pulse of water brought the river up to approx. 5000 cfs.

USGS gage data for that date can be found at: https://waterdata.usgs.gov/ut/nwis/uv?cb_00010=on&cb_00020=on&cb_00060=on&format=gif_default&site_no=09315000&period=&begin_date=2021-06-25&end_date=2021-07-01

How the day unfolded from my journal:

4:58 AM – Matt started swimming before first light, accompanied by a 14′ Wilderness Systems Kayak with 1 person and a 14′ Mad River Canoe with 2 people

5:28 – 1/3 Bobo bar, water

5:55 – waffle, Clif block, electrolytes

6:27 – waffle, block, electrolytes, Vasoline for chafing

6:56 – waffle, water

7:30 – Perpetuem, fig newton

8:30 – Perpetuem, fig newton, block

8:33 – fig newton, electrolytes

9:10 – Honey Stinger, water

9:44 – beef jerky, Gatorade

10:17 – Bobo bar, block, water

10:54 – perpetuem, block

11:06-11:26 AM – Walked across rock/sand bar, warmed up, turkey jerky, water, other food/drink

12:00 – stinger, water

12:30 – electrolyte, block, jerky, water

1:04 – block, fig newton, perpetuem

1:45-2:00 PM – Walked across rock/sand bar, warmed up, chicken and veggies, turkey jerky, water

2:35 – water, block

3:06 – fig newton, water

3:42 – water, waffle

4:12 – perpetuem, waffle

4:47 – Clif, Gatorade

5:20 – stinger, water

6:00 – jerky, water

6:53 – waffle, block, water

7:30-7:40 PM – Exited the river at mile marker 12.3 to discuss stopping. Decided to stop swimming due to low water, darkness and fatigue: 39.6 miles, 14 hours and 32 minutes

Paddled the remaining 12 miles to the confluence of the Green and Colorado rivers, arriving at 11:16 PM

CHRONOLOGY OF SWIMS:

Swimming history can be found at: https://www.openwaterpedia.com/wiki/Matthew_Moseley

Lake Pontchartrain from New Canal Lighthouse to Lake Pontchartrain Yacht Club 24.6 miles in 14 hours and 56 minutes

Colorado River from Potash Point to confluence with Green River, 47 miles/76.4 km in 13 hours and 55 minutes

Culebra (Tamarindo Beach) to Fajardo, Puerto Rico: 24 miles/38 km in 12 hours and 1 minute

Swim Across the Caribbean - St.John to to St Thomas (3 miles) to Culebrita: 24.5 miles in 15 hours

Green River Swim from Mineral Bottom to Mile 12 above confluence: 40 miles in 14 hours and 36 minutes.

Sea of Galilee: North to South, 12.8 miles/20.6 km in 7 hours and 24 minutes

Other Swimming Haunts:

Swim Around Key West - 12.5 miles

Horsetooth Reservoir - 10K

Sayulita to San Pancho, Sayulilta to 8 miles

Golfo Dulce Costa Rica: 21K

Lake Tahoe

SUPPORT CREW:

TO EVERYONE WHO HAS BEEN ON A SUPPORT BOAT

David Amram
Leonard Armijo
Jennifer Bankston
Jonathan Bartsch
Ryan Ballard
Allen Blow
Jennifer Blow
Carolynn Box
Richard Bradley
Dwayne Breashears
Allen Buras
Norb Carr
Sam Carter
Steve Cohn
Mike Dehoff
James Edwards
Enrique Estuldenado
Wayne Ewing
Michael Feduccia
Brian Felse
Jenny Fiebig
Mike Fiebig
Meg Flynn
Tom Giovagnoli
Vicki Goldstein
Anat Grossman
Spencer Hawkins
Uncle Bob and Aunt Karel Howse
George Ingmire
Sky King
John Lopez
Papa Mali (Malcolm Welbourne)
Glynde Mangum

John Mans

J.D.

Pete McBride

Travis McGraw

Amanda McCracken

Amelia Moseley

Charles Moseley

Kristin Moseley

Eli Nieves

Peter Olivo

Rob Putnam

Gad Reich

Matt Rice

Rose Molina Barrios

Stephanie Roaldan

Alfred 'Uganda' Roberts

Coco Robicheaux

Curtis Robinson

Earl and Sue Rogers

Captain Rony

Aaron Rose

Andrew Shoemaker

Randy Soler and Christina Agosto

Stas Stubek

Bud Thompson

Jim Trowbridge

Chad Turner

Pedro and Rose Umpierre

Richard Valadie

Austin Vinton

Kolby Ward

Kyle Ward

Tom Ward

Rick Wiener

Mark Williams

Liza Getches

BIBLIOGRAPHY

Abbey, Edward. *Desert Solitaire: A Season in the Wilderness*. Tucson, University of Arizona Press, 1988.

Ball, Philip. *Life's Matrix: A Biography of Water*. New York, Farrar, Straus and Giroux, 2000.

Barkai, Ram. *From Fire To Ice*. London, Austin Macauley Publishers Ltd, 2022.

Barlow, Maude and Tony Clarke. *Blue Gold: The Battle Against Corporate Theft of the World's Water*. New York, The New Press, 2004.

Belknap, Bill, et al. *Belknap's Waterproof Canyonlands River Guide*. Evergreen, Westwater Books, 2006.

The Bible. Authorized King James Version, Oxford, Oxford University Press, 1998.

Britannica, The Editors of Encyclopaedia. "Kumbh Mela." *Encyclopedia Britannica*, 1 September 2022, www.britannica.com/ topic/Kumbh-Mela. Accessed 2 October 2022.

Byron, George Gordon. "Lord Byron Letter to Henry Drury Salsette Frigate 3 May 1810." *English History*, https://englishhistory.net/byron/selected-letters/henry-drury-salsette-frigate-3-may-1810/. Accessed 8 October 2022.

---. "Written After Swimming From Sestos To Abydos." 1810.

Childs, Craig. *Atlas of a Lost World: Travels in Ice Age America.* New York, Vintage Books, 2019.

Childs, Craig. *House of Rain: Tracking a Vanished Civilization Across the American Southwest.*

Cho, Renee. "Losing Our Coral Reefs." *State of the Planet: News from the Columbia Climate School*, 13 June 2011, news.climate.columbia.edu/2011/06/13/losing-our-coral-reefs. Accessed 8 Oct. 2022.

Conrad, Joseph. *Heart of Darkness and The Secret Sharer.* New York, Signet Classics, 2008.

Cox, Lynne. *Swimming to Antarctica: Tales of a Long-Distance Swimmer.* New York, Houghton Mifflin Harcourt Publishing Company, 2005.

Darwin, Charles. "Letter no. 7471." Darwin Correspondence Project, www.darwinproject.ac.uk/letter/?docId=letters/DCP-LETT-7471.xml. Accessed 4 October 2022.

Dolnick, Edward. *Down the Great Unknown: John Wesley Powell's 1869 Journey of Discovery and Tragedy through the Grand Canyon.* New York, HarperCollins Publishers, 2002.

Emoto Masaru. *The Hidden Messages in Water.* New York, Atria Books, 2005.

Fagan, Brian. *Elixir: A History of Water and Humankind*. New York, Bloomsbury Press, 2011.

Feuerbach, Ludwig. *The Essence of Christianity*. Translated by Marian Evans, London, 1890.

Getches, David H. *Water Law*. St. Paul, West Publishing Co., 1997.

Hemingway, Ernest. *The Old Man and the Sea*. St Albans, Triad Paperbacks Ltd, 1976.

Hemingway, Ernest "The Great Blue River." *Holiday Magazine*, Vol. 6 No. 1, Jul. 1949, pp. 60-63, 95-97.

Isaacson, Walter. *Benjamin Franklin: An American Life*. New York, Simon & Schuster Paperbacks, 2004.

Isaacson Walter. *Leonardo Da Vinci*. New York, Simon & Schuster Paperbacks, 2018.

Johns, Ishbel. "Boston Arrest a Mistake, Says Annette." *Boston Sunday Globe*, 11 October 1953, p. A03.

Kleypas, Joan, et al. "Designing a blueprint for coral reef survival." *Biological Conservation*, Vol. 257, doi: 10.1016/j.biocon.2021.109107.

Kolbert, Elizabeth. "The Lost Canyon Under Lake Powell." *The New Yorker*, 9 August 2021, www.newyorker.com/magazine/2021/08/16/the-lost-canyon-under-lake-powell. Accessed 6 October 2022.

Lopez, Barry. *Desert Notes: Reflections in the Eye of a Raven/River Notes: The Dance of Herons*. New York, Avon Books, 1990.

"Man swims 40 miles of Green River in 14.5 hours." *Times-Independent, The* [Moab, UT], 15 July 2021, www.moabtimes.com/articles/man-swims-40-miles-of-green-river-in-14-5-hours/.

Mányoki, Attila and Martin Schauhuber. *Oceans Seven: How I Cheated Death and Broke theHardest Record in Swimming*. Amazon Publishing, 2021.

McCracken, Amanda. "Matt Moseley's Caribbean Crossing Ends with "The Hardest Swim of My Life." *Men's Journal*, 20 July 2017, www.mensjournal.com/adventure/matt-moseleys-caribbean-crossing-ends-with-the-hardest-swim-of-my-life-w493286/.

McPhee, John. *In Suspect Terrain*. New York, Farrar, Straus and Giroux, 2011.

Means, Howard. *Splash!: 10,000 Years of Swimming*. New York, Hachette Books, 2020.

Melville, Herman. *Moby Dick*. Ware, Wordsworth Editions Limited, 2002.

Moseley, Matthew L. *Ignition: Superior Communication Strategies for Creating Stronger Connections*. Boca Raton, Routledge, 2021.

Interview with Arieh O'Sullivan. "American makes record north-south swim of Sea of Galilee." Israel Public Radio English News, 19 Apr. 2022, https://omny.m/shows/english-news-highlights/american-makes-record-north-south-swim-of-sea-of-g

Munatones, Steve. *Open Water Swimming*. Champaign, Human Kinetics, 2011.

Munatones, Steve. "Swimming Helps Optimize Your Brain Function And Health." *OpenWaterSwimming*, 4 Dec. 2021, World Open Water Swimming Association, www.openwaterswimming.com/swimming-helps-optimize-your-brain-function-and-health/. Accessed 5 October 2022.

Nolan, Heather. "Swimmer reaches north shore after night in the lake - He took on the 25-mile trek to call attention to plight of the wetlands." *Times-Picayune, The* [New Orleans, LA], 13 June 2014, p. A01.

"Alligator pulled from the lake in Mandeville as swimmer nears - It was trying to come ashore." *Times-Picayune, The* [New Orleans, LA], 13 June 2014, p. A08.

Powell, John Wesley. *The Exploration of the Colorado River and its Canyons*. Simon & Brown, 2013.

Rembrandt. *Storm on the Sea of Galilee*. 1633, formerly Isabella Stewart Gardner Museum (stolen), Boston.

Robbins, Jim. "The Godwit's Long, Long Nonstop Journey." *New York Times*, 20 September 2022, www.nytimes.com/2022/

09/20/science/migratory-birds-godwits.html. Accessed 5 October 2022.

Shakespeare, William. *Troilus and Cressida*. Edited by David Bevington, Arden Shakespeare, 1998.

Shelley, Percy Bysshe. "Ode to the West Wind." London, 1820.

Shubin, Neil. *Your Inner Fish: A Journey into the 3.5-Billion-Year History of the Human Body*. New York, Vintage Books, 2009.

Siegel, Seth M. *Let There Be Water: Israel's Solution for a Water-Starved World*. New York, St. Martin's Press, 2015.

Sprawson, Charles. *Haunts of the Black Masseur: The Swimmer as Hero*. Minneapolis, University of Minnesota Press, 2000.

Strong, Douglas Hillman. *Dreamers & Defenders: American Conservationists*. Lincoln, University of Nebraska Press, 1990.

Tennyson, Alfred Tennyson, Baron. *Poems*. 1842.

Thoreau, Henry David. *Walden*. Boston, 1854.

Tsui, Bonnie. *Why We Swim*. Chapel Hill, Algonquin Books of Chapel Hill, 2020.

Twain, Mark. *Life on the Mississippi*. Boston, 1883.

Whitman, Walt. *Leaves of Grass*. New York, 1855.

Whitman, Walt. "Sun-Down Papers No. 1." *The Walt Whitman Archive*, https://whitmanarchive.org/published/periodical/journalism/tei/per.00302.html. Accessed 8 October 2022.

Yanagihara, Hanya. "A Brisk Swim Across Martha's Vineyard." *New York Times*, 4 Feb. 2016, www.nytimes.com/2016/02/04/t-magazine/hanya-yanagihara-swims-marthas-vineyard.html. Accessed 3 Oct. 2022.

Zalasiewicz, Jan and Mark Williams. *Ocean Worlds: The story of seas on Earth and other planets*. New York, Oxford University Press, 2014.

Zoellner, Tom. *Uranium: War, Energy, and the Rock that Shaped the World*. New York, Viking Books, 2009.

BIOGRAPHY:

Matthew L. Moseley is a public affairs and communication strategist, author, speaker and accomplished adventure swimmer. His career has been spent at the intersection of public policy, business and government. He has written several books and is in numerous documentaries. He is the co-chair of the Southwest Regional Board for American Rivers and on the board of the Center for Leadership at the University of Colorado at Boulder. He lives in Boulder, Colorado, with his wife, Kristin, and their children, Charles and Amelia.

ACKNOWLEDGEMENTS:

The writing of the book was a brief capsule compared to the act of living it. Those who were on the adventures and support boats are mentioned in the Support Crew. The people who brought the book to life include:

Holly Neuman, of CG Sports Publishing brought this book from concept to reality, and was the first champion. I am indebted to her dedication and belief in the project. Matt Amerlan, who oversaw production and Nicole Wurtele who designed the cover, layout and the production of the book were fantastic. I express my humble gratitude to Cejih Yung, the founder and leader of CG Sports who makes it all happen.

Elaine Howley was a sharp and insightful editor who understands the history of open water swimming better than anyone. I am grateful for her attention to the details and history of the sport.

I am eternally grateful to my long-time editor Ryan Currasco, the "Book Doctor." He has been a trusted advisor and confidant through the years. It doesn't hurt that he shares my love of New Orleans. He was there from the conception of this book to the final edits.

Many of these adventures would not have happened without Mark Williams, my long time friend and paddler. He has taught me how the mental game is more important than the physical.

My thanks to a number of people read the manuscript through its development, including Colleen Scanlon Lyons, James Edwards and Rosalind Wiseman, Andrew Travers and Christien Shangraw.

I would like to thank those who participated in a live

reading of the book from cover to cover and those who read chapters including Michael Feduccia, Stephanie Roalden, Gad Reich, and as always, my sister Mary Lobdell. Throughout my writing career, she has always been there for me for encouragement, direction and editing.

A hearty *Thank You* to all my friends and colleagues at American Rivers, who work in the trenches of the water conservation movement day in and day out. In particular Matt Rice, who has been a supporter of my swims and work, and Mike Fiebig, who paddled nearly 28,000 paddle strokes alongside me on the Green River.

While I am not a traditional athlete, I have been blessed by some non-traditional sponsors where our partnership is not about moving product, but in moving a message. I have been blessed by many sponsors and supporters including, Beryl Stafford and TJ McIntyre at Bobo's Oat Bars who are longtime friends who have provided fuel for swimming; Mike Boyd and Steve and Christine Case at Nite Ize and who light up my way across the water, the folks at Epics Water Filters who have created cutting edge bottles. My long-time companeroTomas DeFrancia at RovR Product, who creates the coolest coolers on the planet, has always believed in The Dream. Phil Lewis has created majestic art and allowed us to host events at his gallery in Boulder. Chris Wirth of Liberty Puzzles has turned the art into a mind-bending puzzle.

I would also like to thank the Walton Family Foundation, the Inland Ocean Coalition, the Lake Pontchartrain Basin Foundation, 5 Gyres, Wayne Ewing Films, John Mans Production, Dana Franko, Pete McBride, and many others who have contributed one way or another.

Thank you to Liza Getches and Peter Olivo for their friendship and the use of Casa Abuelas, the Writing Tower where her father, the legendary water law professor, David Getches wrote.

Throughout the years, I have been enormously lucky to have

great coaches including Jane Scoot who founded the legendary Boulder Aquatic Masters program and Randy Soler from Puerto Rico. Coach Josiah Middaugh in Vail has been an influential and a guiding force in my training and approach to endurance.

Lastly, to my wife, Kristin, who made this book possible with the original gift of the Mad River canoe and her constant encouragement and support through all of my endeavors. My eternal love and gratitude to our children, Charles and Amelia, who have shared these experiences and developed their own love of rivers.

I have made every attempt to record accurate facts, distances and times.

Thank you to everyone on my support crew everywhere, you know who you are.

Printed in the USA
CPSIA information can be obtained
at www.ICGtesting.com
CBHW051224071223
2267CB00015B/64